The Laughing Guide to a Better Life

The Laughing Guide to a Better Life

*Using Humor and Science to Improve Yourself,
Your Relationships, and
Your Surroundings*

Isaac Prilleltensky and
Ora Prilleltensky

ROWMAN & LITTLEFIELD
Lanham • Boulder • New York • London

Published by Rowman & Littlefield
An imprint of The Rowman & Littlefield Publishing Group, Inc.
4501 Forbes Boulevard, Suite 200, Lanham, Maryland 20706
www.rowman.com

Unit A, Whitacre Mews, 26-34 Stannary Street, London SE11 4AB

British Library Cataloguing in Publication Information Available

Library of Congress Cataloging-in-Publication Data

Names: Prilleltensky, Ora, 1959– author. | Prilleltensky, Isaac, 1959– author.
Title: The laughing guide to a better life : using humor and science to improve yourself, your relationships, and your surroundings / Isaac Prilleltensky, Ora Prilleltensky.
Description: Lanham, Maryland : Rowman & Littlefield, [2019] | Includes bibliographical references and index.
Identifiers: LCCN 2018032964 (print) | LCCN 2018035040 (ebook) | ISBN 9781475846386 (electronic) | ISBN 9781475846379 (cloth : alk. paper)
Subjects: LCSH: Change (Psychology) | Laughter. | Self-realization.
Classification: LCC BF637.C4 (ebook) | LCC BF637.C4 P748 2019 (print) | DDC 158.1—dc23
LC record available at https://lccn.loc.gov/2018032964

∞™ The paper used in this publication meets the minimum requirements of American National Standard for Information Sciences Permanence of Paper for Printed Library Materials, ANSI/NISO Z39.48-1992.

Printed in the United States of America

To Matan and Elizabeth

Contents

Preface

This is the third book in *The Laughing Guides* trilogy. The books are about creating a better life for yourself and others in the community. The first one, *The Laughing Guide to Well-Being*, used humor and science to become happier and healthier. The second, *The Laughing Guide to Change*, focused on mastering three drivers of change: behaviors, emotions, and thoughts. The present book is concerned with improving yourself, your relationships, and your surroundings.

While the first book introduced a research-based theory of well-being, the second and third focus on strategies for change. Each book can be read independently, but you will get the most impact, and the most laughs, by reading them all. You can read them in any order you wish.

The three books use a heavy dose of humor (*the laughing side*), and a healthy measure of science (*the learning side*). In the *laughing side* of each chapter, we review the skills through humor. In general, you'll see that our problems derive from overdoing something or not doing enough of it.

Most neurotics like Isaac tend to worry too much, exercise too much, think about what they eat too much, work too much, plan too much, and overall obsess too much. On the other hand, some folks don't think enough about what they eat, don't pay enough attention to work, and they are overall clueless about their impact on other people. See if you find yourself, or anyone you know, in any of the stories. The motto of this book is *smarter through laughter*. If you can laugh about it, you can probably change it.

Acknowledgments

We gratefully acknowledge the work of our research team in building with us an intervention (www.funforwellness.com) based on the ideas reported in this book. We appreciate the contributions of Samantha Dietz, Adam McMahon, Nick Myers, and Carolyn Rubenstein. We also thank Patrizia Rizzo for help with the references and Yvette Carpintero for general support for Isaac as executive assistant extraordinaire. Michael Lewis of *Miami Today* graciously allowed Isaac to reproduce some humor columns previously published in his weekly newspaper. We also thank our editors at Rowman & Littlefield, Tom Koerner and Carlie Wall, for their support and guidance.

Chapter One

Ease into a Better Life

THE LEARNING SIDE

I CAN Model

The *"I CAN model"* stands for interactions, context, awareness, and next steps. Interactions are powerful determinants of health and happiness.[1] Support from others is often crucial in attaining our goals. Constant criticism and rejection, in turn, prove detrimental to our self-esteem and self-efficacy. There are two skills that can make our interactions healthier: the ability to connect and the capacity to communicate.[2] Family and friends can be our best allies or our worst enemies. We must find ways to assert our needs and engage in reciprocal relationships.

Context is also a powerful but often neglected driver of change. The contexts of our lives consist of people, places, and things. Together, they exert enormous influence on our behavior. Marketing, for example, is all about context: how to sell a particular product, where to place chocolate bars in the supermarket, and what images to use in magazines.

To leverage context to our advantage we need to master the art of reading cues and changing cues. Putting a fruit bowl on the kitchen table is a reminder to eat natural things when we need a sugar kick. Leaving your gym clothes next to your bed is a prompt to exercise first thing in the morning; it's all about our surroundings.[3]

Awareness is the next driver of change. There are two kinds that we should master: know yourself and know the issue.[4] Knowing yourself means being a good detective. Thinking about when I feel best and when I eat worst are good places to start, but to make positive changes, we also need to know something about the issue we're tackling. Am I feeling depressed, am I in a bad relationship, do I feel stuck at work? For every possible challenge you need to tackle there is a wealth of information, and we'll encourage you to become an informed consumer. Do not relinquish control of your life to others. Do your research.

Every step of the way requires a next step. This is why we call the fourth driver of change "next steps." Regardless of where you are in the process of change, there is always a next step to strengthen your change, maintain your gains, and keep thriving. To do that, you need to make a plan, and you need to make it stick.[5] We devote the last chapter to these skills.

When you combine behaviors, emotions, and thoughts, the subject of *The Laughing Guide to Change*, with interactions, context, awareness, and next steps, the subject of this book, you end up with a model called BET I CAN. These seven drivers present many opportunities. I can work on my thoughts, emotions, or behaviors. I can improve my communication skills and my relationships. I can modify my surroundings to make them healthier. I can remove junk food from my house to eliminate temptations. I can increase my awareness about the health benefits of exercise.

Changes in any of the BET I CAN drivers can empower you to make improvements in areas of life that are important to you. The advantage of using BET I CAN drivers is that they occur naturally and don't require major life adjustments. For some people it is easier to change a behavior than a thought. For others, it is a priority to change how they feel or how they interact with others. The point is to experience success in one domain of life to increase your feeling of competency. Once you gain confidence it is easier to tackle other domains where the challenges are bigger.

The key is to engage a driver of change that seems easy, appealing, and you can use to advance a meaningful goal. As you make your way through the books, you'll discover techniques that are easy to implement and follow. While each book in this trilogy can be read independently, we recommend reading the three of them to get a full picture of well-being and the various methods of change. To facilitate learning and application, we broke down each driver into two specific skills:

Behaviors

- Set a goal
- Create positive habits

Emotions

- Cultivate positive emotions
- Manage negative emotions

Thoughts

- Challenge negative assumptions
- Write a new story

Interactions

- Connect
- Communicate

Context

- Read the Cues
- Change the Cues

Awareness

- Know Yourself
- Know the Issue

Next Steps

- Make a plan
- Make it stick

Behaviors, *emotions*, and *thoughts*, are covered in *The Laughing Guide to Change. Interactions, context, awareness,* and *next steps*, are covered in this book. Each chapter deals with a different driver of change and its corresponding skills. In this chapter we provided an overview of the "I CAN" part of the model. The rest of the book is about applying these four drivers of change to improve yourself, your relationships, and your surroundings.

THE LAUGHING SIDE

United in Judgment

Critics of Miami often claim that our city is divided and fragmented. Well, they're wrong. All of us in Miami have something very special in common: We're all judgmental, and if we want to change it, we better become aware of it. Hondurans are critical of Salvadorians, Dominicans fight with Haitians, Cubans don't like to be confused with Puerto Ricans, and the Porteños from Buenos Aires cannot talk to those of us from Córdoba because we're not as erudite, sophisticated, pompous, or pretentious as they are.

But in times of need, we all come together around something we all love in Miami: plastic surgery. When it comes to flesh and flash, we all lower our defenses, show solidarity, and compare prices between Dr. Buttsky and Dr. Bustos.

No doubt, we need more opportunities to suspend judgment and collaborate, which is not easy. Take me, Isaac, for example. I try really hard not to be judgmental of people who are judgmental, but if I don't judge their judgmental attitude, they will continue to judge others, generating in their victims a judgmental attitude that they will perpetuate for generations to come, because, as everybody knows, the apple doesn't fall far from the tree, and silicone implants don't grow on trees.

I believe that change starts within you, which is why I joined Judgmentals Anonymous (JA). After we all recited the prayer and reviewed the 12 steps, it was time for each of us to share our innermost judgmental attitudes. After hearing a litany of sexist, racist, classist, homophobic, ethnocentric, discriminatory, abusive comments about every possible group in Miami, my judgmentalism looked pretty innocuous. "I'm judgmental of people who are judgmental," I said, to which everybody said I'm not being honest.

"Really," I said, "that's my problem, I swear." That did not go down well and they all started judging me for not being honest and insisting that I must harbor some resentment toward some group, some deep-seated hatred. "Otherwise you wouldn't be here," they said. Eventually, they kicked me out of the group for being a phony judgmental, which I thought was the worst kind of judgmentalism.

Puzzled by my dilemmas, I consulted with Dr. Clearhead from the Department of Philosophy at Cambridge University. I wanted to know how to overcome my negative perceptions of people who are judgmental without perpetuating, at the same time, their judgmental attitude by adopting a passive attitude toward their judgmentalism. Dr. Clearhead informed me that this is known as "The Judgmental's Paradox" and that I should try some plastic surgery instead of worrying about silly things.

Dejected by the lack of psychological and philosophical answers to my dilemma, I decided to ask someone who was pragmatic, fair and balanced, so I contacted Fox News. A spokesman for the organization told me that the best way to overcome my paradox is to repeal Obamacare.

I resorted to some introspection. I tried to remember a time when I was the subject of judgmentalism. Perhaps I had some repressed memories that were bugging me. Perhaps the folk in JA were right after all. Without much effort, I recalled the following event, which was, unlike most of the things I write about in this section, true. I was invited to Sydney, Australia, to give a keynote address at a conference. This was soon after I had published a book with a friend on the topic of the conference.

After a long day at the conference, I was invited by some local colleagues to have dinner with them. Not all of us had met before, and no sooner did we sit down than folks started talking about my book. Professor Magnum (not his real name), who did not know that I was the author of the book, started berating my work big time. While others around the table were trying to motion to him that I was right there, sitting in front of him, he kept talking about flaws in the book. When finally somebody whispered to him that I was one of the authors of the book, he turned beet red and tried to get out of it diplomatically.

It's not like I can't handle criticism, but the guy had no idea what he was talking about. He was aggrandizing himself and pompously reciting other authors to show off his knowledge. Never mind that he hasn't published anything of importance himself or ever made the minutest contribution to any field of inquiry. Not to mention he had bad breath. The guy was a pretentious, snobbish, arrogant, and intellectually inferior academic with no original idea of his own. He reminded me of so many others like him who make a career criticizing others instead of doing something useful themselves. These people are intolerable. I tell you, I can't stand them!

I wonder if I could go back to JA now.

Parental Fitness

For those of us who are parents, connecting with your kids is challenging, to say the least. If you're thinking of having children, take this test first. If you already have children, the test will tell you whether you need to: (1) issue a recall, (2) check your mental health, or (3) replace Mother Theresa in the archives of history.

1. Would you enjoy observing your child throw a temper tantrum in the middle of a supermarket?

   a.   Yes, I'm a masochist
   b.   Yes, provided my child has a good reason for it
   c.   No, I rather have a colonoscopy in the woods

2. Do you enjoy feeling guilty?

   a.   Of course, I'm Jewish
   b.   Of course, I'm Catholic.
   c.   Is there any other way?

3. Do you enjoy eating leftover spaghetti dressed with baby snot?

   a.   Yes, my mother never let me eat my snot

b.   Yes, provided it's from my baby's plate

c.   I'm allergic to gluten

4. Would you enjoy worrying about your baby?

a.   I'm petrified

b.   My life is too boring

c.   What's there to worry about?

5. Do you enjoy spending weeks without sleep?

a.   Yes, provided I can watch *Lingerie Football* reruns

b.   Yes, I'd do anything to be near my baby at night when she screams

c.   No, I operate a nuclear reactor in the morning

6. Do you enjoy smelly bedrooms?

a.   I wish I did, but I have anosmia (note to self: google *anosmia*).

b.   In my family, we bond through odors

c.   Ever heard of Febreze?

7. Do you enjoy being ignored?

a.   There is a pill for that

b.   Yes, provided I'm ignored by my precious creature

c.   It depends by whom

8. Would you enjoy driving a group of seven year olds in your van for hours from soccer to Kumon to SAT classes?

a.   Definitely, especially in Miami traffic

b.   How else are they going to get into Harvard?

c.   What am I, a sucker?

9. Do you enjoy gossiping about lousy teachers?

a.   Only about Mrs. Rivera

b.   They deserve it

c.   What else is there to do while we wait for our kids outside school?

10. Do you enjoy talking with kids about the importance of using a condom?

a.   What is a condom?

b.   I'd ask my Rabbi to do it

c.   There is an app for that

11. Would you enjoy getting calls at work from your babysitter that you must run to the emergency room?

a.   It's always good to take a break from work
b.   No big deal
c.   I'm about to faint

12. Do you enjoy cleaning poop?

a.   Yes, my mother never let me play in the sandbox
b.   My baby will be born toilet trained
c.   Where's that stupid app?

13. Do you enjoy punk music?

a.   It's the only kind we play in our house
b.   I'm open minded
c.   I hate it

14. Do you like a neat house?

a.   Are there any other kinds?
b.   I'm OCD
c.   Neat houses are repressive

15. Do you enjoy hosting wild parties?

a.   We never stopped
b.   Anything for our gem
c.   I hate noise

16. Do you enjoy science projects?

a.   I'm a humanist
b.   I'm a rocket scientist
c.   Science is a left-wing conspiracy

17. Do you enjoy self-abnegation?

a.   Self what?
b.   I'm a Jewish mother; is there any other way?
c.   I'm big on selfies of any kind

18. Would you enjoy working until your eighties to fund your child's education?

a.   Ignorance is bliss
b.   Anything for my baby
c.   I hate elitist snobs

19. Would you enjoy seeing your teenage daughter go out with older men with chains and tattoos in a motorcycle squad?

a.   Pass me the Xanax
b.   I ride a Harley-Davidson
c.   I need a therapist

20. Would you enjoy seeing your child in competitive situations?

a.   I cannot bear the thought of my child losing in a competition
b.   It's all about the journey, not the result
c.   My child will never lose

21. Do you enjoy arguing?

a.   It builds character
b.   It drives me crazy
c.   Only against people I can prove wrong

22. Do you enjoy punctuality?

a.   We're German
b.   Punct what?
c.   We're late, stop asking me stupid questions

23. Do you enjoy feeling insecure?

a.   It's my favorite state
b.   I wish I knew anything else
c.   I voted for Donald Trump

If you answered mostly b, you're ready to be a parent and to be admitted to the nearest sanatorium. If you answered mostly a, you might be able to be a parent *after* you're admitted to the nearest sanatorium. If you answered mostly c, you're in a sanatorium, and I hope you never have children, especially if you operate a nuclear reactor.

Immanuel Kant was totally wrong. Human beings are the most irrational species on the face of the earth. Before our son was born, there was order in my world. I used to get up at a certain time, eat breakfast at a certain time, and go to the toilet at a certain time. My life was a sanatorium: orderly, clean, and predictable, with a fresh scent of Febreze. I was happy. The arrival of our beloved son changed all that, especially the orderly thing. Order turned into chaos, predictability into pandemonium, and Febreze into acrid vomit. Nobody should undermine the adorability factor of babies. Without it, it would all be too much to bear, especially for sanatorium lovers.

I cannot be faulted for feeling a little insecure about my parenting from time to time. When Ora and I attended Lamaze classes, I used to fall asleep. It was so relaxing that after a full day at work, I really enjoyed the nap. When we were in the delivery room, Ora told the head nurse that "my husband is very supportive, but has no idea how to do the breathing." Grabbing Ora's hand, Mama Nurse said, "Don't worry honey, I'm right here." Ora breathed a big sigh of relief. I never recovered.

On a scale of 1 to a 100, Ora scores 99 for guilt. Happy-go-lucky me: 98. On the worry scale, Ora is a 100; me, the free-spirit, 99. When our son Matan got married to Elizabeth, Ora organized part of the honeymoon in Greece with Elizabeth's mom. Between the two mothers, they booked hotels, ferry tickets, and taxis.

With internet and what not, Ora communicated via email with a taxi driver in Greece. Abraxas was supposed to pick up the kids from their hotel in Athens and take them to the port to catch the Santorini ferry. To make sure the driver picked them up on time, Ora sent him multiple email reminders. Abraxas emailed promptly, confirming delivery of the two kids. Ora wanted a picture of the newlyweds actually boarding the ferry, but I intervened.

The pinnacle of my guilt was when "the child," twenty-two years old at the time, flew to Toronto from Miami for a chess tournament. We did not have U.S. passports yet, so he used his Canadian passport to fly there. That was no problem, but when he wanted to get back to the United States, the customs officer in Toronto requested to see Matan's green card, which I had forgotten to give him. That it was *my fault* there was no doubt. Nobody in our house is supposed to worry about little details like that. Matan phoned from the airport to share the news. "I'm stuck in the Toronto airport." For him, it was a good story, and an opportunity to have an extra night at a nice hotel. For me, it was a certificate of failure. I could not FedEx the green card fast enough to deal with my guilt.

On neatness, Ora scores 7, which is 93 points less than me. To contain the mess when Matan was young, we lived in houses with basements. There we had big, carpeted family rooms, with wall-to-wall toys strewn everywhere, but mostly out of my sight. From time to time though, it would all be too much to bear and I'd organize everything in boxes.

The Matchbox cars gave me the most work. For a while, Matan was obsessed with miniature cars. He had about 200 of them, and he knew the make and model of every single one. This he learned from Eleanor, his babysitter, who used to sit with him on the porch and teach him about all the cars passing by.

With his phenomenal memory, Matan could identify all the domestic and foreign cars made between 1965 to 1990, and he was not shy about telling one and all what he knew, not just about cars, but about everything and anything, since he was about nine months old. On the love of silence, I'm a 100. I realized that I had some growing up to do, but lucky for us, when Matan was eight years old, he discovered chess, a game that requires a lot of quiet.

On the competitiveness scale, Ora and I are a cool 15 out of a 100. We love seeing our son win chess tournaments, but we really supported him for the journey and not for the trophies. He made lots of friends through chess, developed a wonderful hobby—which turned into a career—and found an amazing outlet for his energy and brain power. Of all the mistakes we probably made as parents, putting pressure on him to win games was not one of them. We loved taking him to tournaments and, over time, watching him blossom into an independent, self-assured young man.

The Primrose Hotel in Toronto was a frequent weekend destination. Leaving the house on time to make the seventy-five-minute trip on the 401 was always an ordeal, but once we got there—usually at the last minute—Matan kissed us goodbye and promptly disappeared into chess bliss. It was quite a sight. Hundreds of kids lined up on both sides of chess boards, along tables that spanned the whole width of the ballroom.

We were quite anxious during the first tournament. It was hard to spot him among the sea of children, and we did not want to walk by the aisles and disturb the players. At first, we would stay right by the door of the ballroom, to make sure he found us if needed (he never did). With us, were many East Indian, Chinese, Caribbean, Russian, Anglo, Jewish, and Filipino parents waiting in the lobby for updates.

With time, we became comfortable enough to leave the hotel. We got to know every coffee shop in downtown Toronto, not to mention the charming neighborhoods and ethnic restaurants. But unlike us, some parents were 100 on the competitiveness scale and would not leave their children alone.

During the very first tournament at the Primrose, Matan played his last game against a boy whose parents were a stress ball. As Matan won the game, we witnessed the parents giving their son such a hard time that it was really painful to watch. It was as if family honor, and the whole Russian chess dynasty hung in the balance.

Add to the adorability factor sportsmanship. In the twenty-two years since Matan has been playing chess, he has never begrudged an opponent for beating him. Matan is gracious, courteous, friendly, and positive. On the optimism scale, he is a 100. The sun always shines for Matan, but not everyone has the same attitude.

When we lived in Australia, we were visiting Sydney and came upon a large-scale chess set in a park. As Matan was inspecting the set, a guy in a suit and tie challenged him to a game. Ora and I observed from a distance, and could see that the guy was not doing well.

The game went on for a while, and although the well-dressed dude put up a good fight, he lost to Matan, who would have been twelve years old at the time. Before leaving, the guy told us that he "lets children win sometimes." That was the worst incarnation of the poor loser. I feel for his children. In fact, I hope he doesn't have any. How dare he put down my kid? I hope he's still suffering from that defeat, and that he never gets a promotion, and that he develops hemorrhoids.

Chess is a difficult sport. It takes a lifetime to improve, and if you want to get better, you have to play against serious players, who will often beat you, time and again. But Matan was constantly willing to play up. He always wanted a challenge, and he never failed to learn from mistakes. He taught chess at a couple of schools in New York City, and his students won regional and national tournaments every year. He is adored by students, parents, and peers.

On the love of arguing scale, I'm a 1. I shy away from conflict. I'm a peacemaker. It takes just too much time to argue, and even more to make up, not to mention the usual pain associated with saying "I'm sorry for losing my cool." On the perfectionism scale, I'm a 100. Coming to terms with losing my cool was incompatible with my self-image of calm, cool, and collected. These were my trademarks B.C. (before child).

Although Matan chose chess as a career, he was born a debater. We had endless arguments about cleaning his room now or later, leaving the house for the Toronto tournament at 8:00 a.m. or 8:05 a.m., about doing homework at 7:00 p.m. or 7:03 p.m. And since we never used corporal punishment and tried really hard to use respectful language, the only means available to us to impose some discipline was to talk, which only played to his strengths.

Once, we were at a playground in Kitchener, Ontario, trying to eliminate his fear of slides. Matan, four at the time, would climb the ladder alright, but lecture us from the top about why it's not a good idea for him to go down the slide. He'd give us long-winded arguments about the risks involved. Eventually we imposed a "no talking" rule, and he learned to come down the slide.

Matan has provided us with years of entertaining impersonations, stories about chess characters, and most recently, teaching experiences. Sometimes he calls us but cannot talk because he is laughing so hard. No opportunity to laugh goes wasted. For a while, Matan started calling me Muhammad. That was the name of the chef at his college cafeteria. The person attending the counter was Ahmed. Matan loved how Ahmed used to shout orders to the chef: "MUHAMMAAAAAAD, two fried eggs," "MUHAMMAAAAAAD, an order of humus." Although Matan does not speak Arabic, he could imitate the accent very well.

Matan grew very fond of both Ahmed and Muhammad. Soon enough, I started getting emails and texts from Matan addressing me as Muhammad. I would oblige by replying "what's happening, Ahmed?" Ora was also in the know, addressing us as Ahmed and Muhammad. This went on for a while. On a visit to New York, Ora and I went into a shoe store and began our routine. Ora looked for shoes while I looked grumpy—my natural state of affairs in stores. Then, all of a sudden I saw that employees assisting customers had name badges. That is not unusual, but two of the guys were named Ahmed and Muhammad! Right then and there, without hesitation, I shouted: "MUHAMMAAAAAD, can you call Ahmed to give me a hand with some shoes." Ora thought that I had lost my mind, but I could not wait to tell Matan.

But if his Arabic impressions are good, his Yiddish and Hebrew impersonations are even better. To speak Yiddish, as Billy Crystal noted, you must be able to mimic phlegm, which both Matan and I enjoyed doing while looking for houses in Melbourne, Australia. Poor Matan was bored out of his mind. We had just arrived in Australia, and were looking to buy in Caulfield, the Jewish enclave. Since he was only twelve years old, and we did not know anybody, we could not leave him alone or drop him off somewhere, so we dragged him to look at real estate. Nothing could be more punishing for him until we started impersonating the Jewish sellers and real estate agents. We would return to the car after an inspection, close the door, and Matan would yell, in phlegmy Yiddish, "Mrs. Zilberger, are you Jewish?"

While humor compensates for the irrational behavior of human beings in procreating, there are no guarantees that your children will get it. In my family of origin, we had a fifty-fifty chance. My mom was a 100 on the competitiveness scale, and she was not kidding. She would call my aunt every afternoon to find out what grades my cousin Sissi got in school, only to put down my brother Mario for not measuring up to our cousin. No sooner would my brother get off the school bus than my mother would yell at him for not being as good as Sissi.

My mom was not just competitive. She was freakishly neat. My two siblings and I could not play in the dirt, mud, sand, or gravel, unless we returned home with our clothes washed and ironed. To make sure there were no shoe marks on the floor, we had to slide on pieces of felt over the wooden floors. These pieces of felt, ubiquitous in Argentina, were known as "patines." Every one of our aunts and uncles had them by the door. Truth be told, my mom was pretty stern.

My dad, however, was a funny guy. He was a salesman for a while, traveling by car to remote parts of Argentina selling clothes. As there was no TV at the time, and few publications reached remote areas of the country, some people didn't know what celebrities looked like. My dad would delight us with stories about pretending to be Carlos Gardel and garnering the admiration of the locals in Catamarca, La Rioja, and San Juan. My two siblings and I have a decent sense of humor, but remember there are no guarantees. Instead of asking Muhammad to call Ahmed for help with shoes, I could have been asking him for patines.

But the key to parenting is not humor, but patience; one of the many qualities I was not born with. I usually finish tasks before they're assigned, and expect others to do the same. Matan, on the other hand, would rarely start assignments until after they were due, but if you develop patience, and wait long enough, you see your kids mature, become responsible adults, and—poetic justice —become teachers!

There is little doubt that if you get along with your kids, you can get along with many others. As we shall see later, you need to master two specific skills to achieve good relationships: how to connect and how to communicate. Humor and patience will help you with both.

Taming Temptations

People undermine the impact of the environment on well-being. The context of our lives is full of temptations, which is why it's so important to read cues and change cues. There are cues calling on us all around us. These environmental cues are like subliminal commands: "Buy me," "take me home," "drink me," Consider the following:

Scene 1

Trigger situation: Charlie needs toilet paper. He drives to the nearest pharmacy.

Charlie's self-talk: I'll just buy toilet paper. I don't need anything else.
Behavior: Charlie wastes two hours at the pharmacy and spends $879 on stuff he doesn't really need. He forgets toilet paper.
Consequence: Charlie goes bankrupt without toilet paper.

Scene 2

Trigger situation: Fred is bombarded by Viagra ads.

Fred's self-talk: I don't need this, I don't have erectile dysfunction.
Behavior: Fred goes to the pharmacy and gets eight packs of Viagra.
Consequence: Fred gets an erection lasting seven hours. He misses work and gets fired.

Scene 3

Trigger situation: Sofia drives south on the Palmetto Highway every day to go to work. She passes through Dr. Buttsky's Plastic Surgery Clinic. Buttsky displays on an electronic board some of the butts he has sculpted over the years.

Sofia's self-talk: Gosh, who needs that?
Behavior: Sofia decides to have a Brazilian butt lift at Dr. Buttsky's clinic. Her butt is displayed on electronic boards across South Florida.
Consequence: Sofia becomes so sexy that she decides to dump her husband.

Scene 4

Trigger situation: Greg is at the buffet on a cruise.

Greg's self-talk: I can handle all this temptation. I know better.
Behavior: Greg loads up his plate with six different cakes oozing LDL for six consecutive days, twice a day.
Consequence: His cholesterol goes up to 800. There isn't enough Lipitor in the world to save him. His life insurance is revoked. He collapses of a massive heart attack and his family is destitute for generations to come.

Scene 5

Trigger Situation: Mark goes to a bar with his buddies.

Mark's self-talk: I know my limits.
Behavior: Mark gets wasted out of his mind.
Consequence: He gets up three days later, in another city. He misses work and gets fired.

While stores, cruise lines, breweries, and Dr. Buttsky are laughing their way to the bank, Charlie, Sofia, Greg, Mark, and Fred have totally ruined their lives. They could have prevented all of this, but no, they thought that the environment doesn't influence them. They thought that signs cannot impact their behavior and that surroundings don't matter. They thought that their willpower was stronger than that. They thought that they could handle temptations. They thought they were masters of self-discipline.

So, what's the solution? First, stop kidding ourselves. We're all suckers. Once we realize that the environment is full of temptations, 99 percent of which are bad for us, we can begin changing the context so we're not tempted.

I know that my family is not an example of anything other than utter neurosis, but I have never allowed my cholesterol to go over 200 (although I have thought of a Brazilian butt lift). Still, in my house you'll never find junk food, sugar, milk, meat, cakes, alcohol, sodas, or white bread. Come to think of it, I don't know what the heck we do eat, but I can tell you that we're pretty healthy, and that my life insurance has never been revoked, and I've never brought shame to my family, here or abroad.

Planning Interruptus

Cacophony; that's it, this is what our lives have become. Instead of a melodious and carefully orchestrated sequence of planned events, our lives have turned into a random series of occurrences driven by immediate gratification and digital sounds, which is what the twenty-first century will be remembered for. To say nothing of the fact that I always wanted to say cacophony, which gets in the way of any planning at all.

There was a time when you could isolate yourself and engage in some thinking or planning. You could set a goal and try to pursue it through a series of rational steps. Today, you're lucky if you get 30 seconds of peace and quiet before your telephone beeps, your email alert pops up, and your electronic calendar reminds you to check Facebook, lest your friend has diarrhea and you're the last one to know.

Instead of thinking about our future and planning ways to achieve it, we spend countless hours searching for the miracle app that will replace our thinking and doing. What's more, there are tons of start-ups devising these apps and convincing you that their products will do the hard work for you. Well, I have news for you. I developed such an app too, which took a lot of planning and cacophony, but I'll spare you the details. After all, I had planned on writing a piece about planning, not apps. Where were we?

To improve your well-being, you need to resist immediate gratification and cacophony. This means turning your phone off, not just airplane mode, but completely off. Go ahead. Try it. Millions of people before 1992, when the first smart phone was introduced, had done it. Now shut off your tablet, your laptop, and your Apple watch and any other devices such as Fitbits and Vitamixes. When you stop twitching from withdrawal, you're ready to think about a goal you want to pursue. If you cannot keep your hands off your phone, tablet, remote, or desktop, you may need to join a Buddhist monastery in Bhutan, where there is no cable or Wi-Fi.

Once you overcome your addiction to digital devices and your twitching subsides, you're ready for the next challenge: be by yourself. No talking. No singing. No selfying. Just be quiet. If this is hard, you can say either ohm or cacophony a few times, sotto voce. Now you have to think. I know that this may sound strange. After all, your tablet, laptop, remote, and internet have been doing all the thinking for you for the last ten years.

Let me tell you how thinking works. If no thoughts come to mind, check your pulse. If you still have a pulse, try to ask yourself questions: what do I want to accomplish in life, what type of person do I want to become, what is going to be my legacy, how can I help humanity, how can I improve my life, how often should I change my underwear? If no questions come to mind, check your pulse again. Try controlling your twitching.

Then try to create a plan for achieving your goals. If you want to reduce stress in your life, getting a one-way ticket to Bhutan is a good first step. If you don't have a passport, think of beeping devices you can eliminate from your life. Then think of apps you can delete.

Perhaps you want to lose weight instead of reducing your stress. There are many apps for that. Go ahead and delete them all. Yes, all of them. Now throw away all the diet books you have at home. C'mon. That should not be too hard. After all, you've barely read them. No phones, no apps, no computer, no books.

Now, go ahead and disconnect your TV. I know this is hard because this is your main meaning-making activity, but for you to set goals and pursue them, you need to minimize distractions. If you know what a radio is, and own one, unplug it. Now you will face silence. You may not know what silence is, but let it wash over you.

It is possible that, despite your good intentions to enjoy peace and quiet, some moron near you is talking on the phone so loudly that you need to get a Bose noise cancelation device. Pretty soon everyone will have to walk around with one, just to avoid the cacophony of nonsense emitted by people who have nothing better to do than to broadcast to the whole world their inane and stupid whereabouts. Not to mention fights with their ex over the phone, in public spaces, such as bathroom stalls, airports, trains, bus stops, shopping centers, medical examination rooms, fitting rooms, and movie theaters.

Airplanes are the worst, since there is nowhere to hide. No sooner the plane lands than 99 percent of passengers reach for their smartphones to continue sharing with their best friend scintillating details about their day: got up around 6:30 a.m., had my coffee, read the paper, farted.

The addiction to digital devices is so great that some folks are now taking their laptops to the gym with them. At our previous condo, where I usually could expect peace and quiet in the exercise room, there appeared a guest who was in the rather small exercise room with his three-year-old and a laptop. I could live with the kid walking around the fitness equipment, but his father's laptop was playing a video of a fitness instructor yelling at the top of his lungs invocations such as "Does it hurt now?" "Do you want to be a man?" "Do it! Do it! Be a man! Lift, lift, lift!" The father was following every word and every movement of the fitness guru.

As the intruder saw me coming into the small gym, he asked if I mind the noise from the laptop, to which I said yes. He proceeded to tell me that the video will motivate me and will be good for me. One of the last sanctuaries of peace and quiet, our condo gym, which is frequented only by senior citizens thirty years older than me, was transformed by some digitally addicted brainless creature into a high-decibel motivational class.

If you manage to find a quiet spot, which can be a challenge, then think of what you need to do to become happier, healthier, wealthier, and sexier. No shortcuts. No plastic surgery. What will make you happier? Better relationships? More time with your spouse, with your kids?

Step one would be to stop looking at your phone every five seconds. Then think of asking them open ended questions, such as "What can I do to make your day today?" At first they will think that you're totally out of your mind. Then they will confirm that you're totally out of your mind. This will happen a few times, until they realize that you mean it.

Now let's say you want to improve your nutritional habits. First, set a realistic goal. Then, ask for help. Tell your friends at work not to tempt you with donuts and candy. At first, they will think that you're weird. They will think that for a while. Eventually, you will embrace weird. Weird is nice. Weird is unique. Weird is quiet, independent, and mindful.

The first step in any project is always the hardest, usually because people expect immediate results and instantaneous cure. The key, once you're quiet, and focused, and unplugged—like billions of people before the internet era used to do—is to simplify. Every major undertaking consists of a series of small and achievable steps. Projects don't always work according to plan, but the mere act of planning and thinking is vital, otherwise you have no idea where you're going. As Lewis Carroll said, if you don't know where you're going, any road will take you there. As far as clichés go, you have to admit that this is a good one.

After you have found a quiet spot, reflected on your life, identified a goal, and planned the next step, it is time to actually take that step. Consider all the environmental arrangements you can design in order to make that first step as easy as possible. If you pursue regularity, bring home high-fiber food and stop eating so much white bread. Put a big bowl of high-fiber cereal with prunes on the kitchen table the night before so it's ready for breakfast. If you want to be kind to your kids, write them a love note for their lunchbox the night before, so you don't forget. Some people may say that this is hardly the way to achieve existential meaning, but it will surely put a smile on your kids' face.

Once you have taken the first step, celebrate. Reward yourself for doing something productive. The greatest barrier you will encounter in your pursuit of change is all the noise and visual stimulation around you. As a species, we have an evolutionary task to fulfill. At this rate, our fingers will grow thinner to master small keyboards, and our eyes will begin protruding to read small print on smartphones. All the while our brains are shrinking.

Evolution is about adaptation to the environment. In modern life, we're using our fingers and eyes more than our brains and hearts. If we want to retain, let alone grow the size of our brains, we better switch off the digital noise. Otherwise, evolution will make us into a bunch of ETs.

But planning can be overdone. Speaking from experience, I have spent more time in my life planning than actually living. As an insecure, mildly paranoid, neurotic, orphan, self-conscious Jew, I spent considerable time over many years striving for certainty and security in my life. I spent so much time planning that I had barely any time to enjoy the fruits of my planning, but I had a plan to stop all that planning. Instead of planning, I started writing pointless stories. The fact that you're reading these stories shows two things: (1) I'm succeeding at my plan to spend less time planning, and (2) you have no plans whatsoever.

For being so neurotic and obsessive compulsive, sometimes I surprise myself at how impulsive I can be. In 1999, I was invited to a conference in Sydney, Australia. Soon after I landed I called Ora back in Canada to let her know that we were moving to Australia. This was my first time in Australia, and I absolutely fell in love with it.

Within five months, my family moved to Melbourne, which we loved. There was no planning involved other than the plan to be open to surprises. For a while, I enjoyed the laid-back Aussie style, but after some time my neuroses called home. ET go home.

Looking back, the most successful plan I ever executed was to convince my wife of thirty-five years to marry me. With her we brought to the world the funniest, smartest, most spirited, kindest mensch every Jewish parent would ever want. Both Ora and Matan put up with my obsessive compulsive needs to plan everything, and move continents every so often, and we all do it with a laugh, sometimes planned, sometimes unplanned. Our plans are often interrupted, but our laughter never is.

Chapter Two

Mastering Awareness
to Improve Yourself

THE LEARNING SIDE

To promote our personal well-being, we need to know ourselves and we need to know what we're dealing with. In short, we call it *know yourself* and *know the issue*. In a sense, knowing ourselves is about knowing our own behaviors, emotions, thoughts, interactions, and context of our life.

Know Yourself

Knowing yourself requires a bit of detective work. It is about knowing what values you stand for, and what principles guide your life. But it is also about reflecting on your behaviors, emotions, thoughts, interactions, and context. These drivers of change can tell you if your life is aligned with your values or not. If you behave in ways that betray your value of caring and compassion toward your kids, you're misaligned. If you cherish peace and quiet but you're always feeling stressed, you're out of kilter.

To reach congruence, you need to start with an inventory of your values. This is about knowing what values provide meaning to your life. Unless you know that, you won't know whether you're going in the right direction.

Think about What's Important

What do you value most in life? What gives your life meaning? Is the way you live your life consistent with what is most important to you? If there is a gap between your values and your actions, what can you do to address it?

We all know that our time on this earth is limited and that we will eventually die. In the cosmic sense, we're on this earth but for a very short period of time. Even though we all know this, we sometimes behave as though we have all the time in the world. How we spend our time and the things we worry about on a daily basis do not necessarily reflect our most deeply held values and priorities.

People who experience life-threatening illnesses or other life altering events often comment on how their life has changed as a result. Facing the finality of life has provided them with a new perspective on what is truly important. They often credit such experiences with a shift in priorities and with taking action that is more consistent with their values.

You may value autonomy, freedom, integrity, loyalty, honesty, and hard work. Or perhaps you cherish values like compassion, fairness, equality, solidarity, inclusion, and justice. You may not have asked yourself this question lately, but it's worth it. Create a short inventory of the five most important values that guide your life. Below the name of the value, offer a brief description of why it's important to you. Remember, values are ethical or moral principles that guide your life and your decisions.

Value #1: _____

Why it's important to me:

_____

_____

Value #2: _____

Why it's important to me:

_____

_____

Value #3: _____

Why it's important to me:

_____

_____

Value #4: _____

Why it's important to me:

_____

_____

Value #5: _____

Why it's important to me:

_____

_____

You're now in a position to determine if your actions are aligned with your values. This requires honesty and self-reflection. Are your behaviors in line with your moral principles? Is the work you do congruent with your beliefs about a fair and just world? Do you relate to other people in respectful ways? Do you practice self-compassion? Are you leading the life you hoped for? Your own well-being and the well-being of others depend on the answers. You may be kind to others, but not to yourself. You may be kind to yourself, but not to others.

To help you reach deeper levels of self-understanding, we recommend the following exercise. First, list behaviors that are aligned with any of your values:

Behaviors aligned with my values:

- First: _____

- Second: _____

- Third: _____

- Fourth: _____

Looking at the list, do you feel proud? Do you feel a sense of personal integrity? To be a great detective, you have to ask the opposite question as well: Are there any behaviors that are not well aligned with my values? For example, if you cherish caring and compassion but you're always yelling at people, what do you learn from that? Try this exercise:

Behaviors that are not aligned with my values:

- First: _____

- Second: _____

- Third: _____

- Fourth: _____

It is very hard to achieve full alignment between all our behaviors and all our values. We're not perfect beings, but that shouldn't detract us from trying to get better. If you value health and well-being, but you engage in binge drinking often, that should sound an alert, shouldn't it? If you value dignity and respect, but you find yourself berating coworkers, what is that telling you?

Think about End of Life

Imagine that you're now at the end of life and you look back at how you conducted yourself and what you have accomplished. As you look back, what are you proud of? What are you not proud of? What, if anything, do you wish you did differently? Is the way you lead your life today consistent with what would make you proud? How can this inform your life at present?

In addition to positive emotions and loving relationships, most people yearn for something greater than themselves. We obtain a sense of meaning and purpose by feeling that we're contributing not just to ourselves but to a greater cause. Many people obtain this transcendence through religion and spirituality. Others become involved in various causes for the betterment of others and society at large.

Build on Your Strengths

To achieve higher levels of well-being, some people need to deal with obstacles such as workplace stress, unhealthy eating habits, or toxic environments. Others, who have most of their basic needs met, hope to flourish and thrive, not just exist in a state of pleasant complacency. We all start the pursuit of a better life from a different place, depending on the circumstances of our lives. Some try to minimize pain. Others try to maximize pleasure and purpose. Yet others try to do both at the same time. But regardless of your unique situation, and your particular goal, we think it's valuable to build on your strengths.

Strengths are unique characteristics or experiences that make you resilient to adversity and prone to flourishing. When you deal with problems in successful ways you build your repertoire of coping strategies. When you practice your strengths frequently you enhance your happiness. You may or may not be aware of all your strengths. If you are not, you may want to try the Values in Action (VIA) survey, freely available at www.viacharacter.org.

We all have strengths, and the VIA survey can make you more aware of your unique talents. In my case (Isaac), humor came at the top of the list, followed by love of learning, perseverance, curiosity, and self-regulation. I have to admit that the results of the survey concur very well with my own perceptions. I call upon humor, learning, and perseverance to deal with challenges and find pleasure. The survey provides you with a profile of 24 strengths, in rank order. Try it.

In my personal case, I did not capitalize on my sense of humor until a few years ago, when I started writing funny stories for the newspapers. Eventually the stories made their way to my books. You be the judge if my funny stories make you laugh, but I have a very good time writing them.

Strengths are ways of approaching life and its many challenges. I know that I tackle difficulties with perseverance, love of learning, and self-regulation. They have served me well. What is helping you?

When you think about how to use your strengths, it's helpful to consider the six domains of life we call I COPPE: interpersonal, community, occupational, physical, psychological, and economic.[1] Pick one area in which you either wish to alleviate discomfort or seek higher levels of satisfaction. Let's say you choose to improve your life in the psychological domain. Here you can strive for better emotional or spiritual well-being.

Once you identify some of your key strengths, see if you can apply them to a particular struggle. The first question you can ask yourself is "How have I dealt successfully with this situation before?" If you are feeling somewhat anxious or depressed, can you think of a situation in which you handled these feelings successfully? What did you do to overcome anxiety? Did you talk to yourself? Did you remind yourself that from time to time you suffer from anxiety but that it eventually passes and you feel okay again? Did you go for a walk when you felt somewhat despondent? Who did you talk to? What did you do, think, or feel that alleviated the anxiety?

If you are struggling at work with interpersonal conflict, what personal strength can help you deal with it? Perhaps you are high on forgiveness and empathy. Can you try to put yourself in the shoes of the person you are having a conflict with? Can you try to see the situation from her perspective? Have you used humor before to diffuse tension in a meeting?

All of us experience pain from time to time; physical, relational, or psychological. It is quite inevitable. In addition to using your strengths to cope with the situation, it is important to accept that pain is a normal part of life.[2] Relatives get sick, friends die, you lose your job, or your child gets rejected from the college of his choice. Learning to accept that pain is a part of life can itself become a strength. This is not to say, however, that we should resign ourselves to suffering.

The values you identified in the previous section are a compass for you. They dictate the type of life you want to lead, and the type of person you want to become. If you want to increase your happiness and help others lead meaningful lives, you need to choose a certain path and a particular lifestyle. If getting healthier and helping others are not just chores, but part of your mission in life, then enacting these behaviors is part of living a meaningful life. Once you have clarity with respect to your values and your mission, it is time to do something.

If the task looks overwhelming, remember that every major accomplishment needs to be broken down into small chunks. A long marathon starts with the first step. You can ask yourself, what is the smallest step I can take to achieve happiness, meaning, and health? If your values include kindness and respect toward others, ask yourself what small action you can take to live these values every day.

Getting clarity on your values and personal mission is the first step. Reflecting on what you already do well is the second step. The next phase is accepting that life does not always behave according to plan and that we have to accept challenges. What follows is taking action. You can take behavioral, cognitive, or emotional actions.

From a behavioral point of view, you can *set a goal* such as exercising, spending more time with your kids, or refraining from email during meals. Make sure the goal is specific, measurable, achievable, relevant, and time limited. These are the essentials of a SMART goal.

You can also create a *positive habit.* Habits convert your values and ideals into repeatable actions. In the end, your life is a sequence of habits. If you want to become physically fit, one trip to the gym will not suffice. Not even two, or three. If you are serious about physical wellness, making a habit of moving around will translate aspiration into lifestyle.

From an emotional point of view, you can improve your life by *increasing your positive emotions.* It is not enough to combat negative feelings, you also need to augment positive feelings like laughter, gratitude, forgiveness, and hope. Find opportunities to savor and relish a good experience. Take time to savor the moment. Press the pause button and enjoy your surroundings. Pay attention to beauty in nature. Take time to read a book to your kids. Invite your family to a nature trip.

These feelings should not wait until life is perfect, the mortgage is paid, and you get the coveted promotion. Collecting positive emotions is not something you do after life is in great shape. These experiences will actually help you get into great shape.

From a cognitive point of view, there are certain thoughts that can help you improve your life. *Challenging negative assumptions* is helpful. If you encounter failure at work or at school, there are different explanations that can account for the situation. Stories that (a) blame yourself for the failure, (b) predict that the failure will generalize to other aspects of your life, and (c) anticipate that you will always fail, are seriously harmful.

We should stay away from stories of self-blame. Instead, we should learn from experiences of failure. To do so, we need to embrace a growth mind-set.[3] This is a thinking schema that says the following: (a) there is no learning without failure, (b) the effort and the journey are more important than the outcome, and (c) the process of learning will make me a better and stronger person. Growth mind-sets challenge fixed mindsets. The latter lead you to think that (a) *I'm not good enough, and* (b) *I will always fail, no matter what aspect of my life we're talking about, because this is the way I am.* Embracing a growth mind-set will help you *write a new story* about your life, a story of effort, learning, growth, and challenge.

We have to learn to treat thoughts as thoughts, and not as immutable realities that will kill or maim us. Thoughts can provoke anxiety and fear, but they cannot harm us. We can learn to treat them as events that come and go. We can detach ourselves from these negative thoughts. We do not need to be fused with our thoughts. We do not have to become one with them.

Behaviors, emotions, and thoughts are helpful in two ways: to alleviate pain, and to thrive. Focusing on your strengths will help you achieve higher levels of satisfaction, pleasure, and meaning. In my case, I experienced a new level of pleasure and purpose when I started writing humor. For you, it may be painting, playing a musical instrument, or volunteering in the community.

Becoming aware of our challenges, moving forward with strengths, taking small steps, accepting pain as part of life, and learning from experiences are helpful ways to reduce negative feelings and augment positive ones. Leveraging our behaviors, emotions, and thoughts will promote a value-based life.

Monitor Your Stress

We all strive to lead a meaningful life. We want to feel that we can make a difference and that we're valued. In short, we want to feel that we matter to those around us. Unfortunately, stress gets in the way of thinking about what really matters to us and how we matter to others.

When we experience a threat to our safety and believe we're in danger, our bodies mobilize for action. Our heart pumps more blood, our veins expand, and our pupils dilate to sharpen our vision. This so-called *fight or flight response* can protect us in times of imminent threat. We focus on the source of danger and are well-positioned to either attack an aggressor or flee the situation. The fight or flight response can clearly protect us in the face of imminent danger. The problem is that it can also be activated when there is no danger whatsoever.

Think about the last time that you experienced a fight or flight response. What triggered this reaction? Was there an actual danger to your health and safety? How did you deal with this situation? Did you utilize any strategies that helped you calm down and return to baseline?

Stress is a part of life and we cannot eliminate it altogether. In fact, even positive events like getting married or starting a new job can generate some stress. When we face an external stressor but feel that we have strategies for managing it, we're not overwhelmed with stress. On the other hand, even minor events can be perceived as stressful if we feel that we do not have the capacity to handle them. In other words, the way we frame the situation to ourselves is critical.

Most stress management experts suggest three main ways of dealing with stress. We can either take action to change the situation, change how we think about it, or take steps to manage our emotions.[4] If the situation is not within your control, you can still have control over how you think about it or how you respond on an emotional level.

Consider the Benefits of Mindfulness

Have you ever found yourself scratching your head after flying off the handle? Or catch yourself thinking about something completely unrelated to what you're currently doing? Many of us are so busy getting through the day that we go from one activity to the next without fully inhabiting our present experience. In our minds, we're often busy planning or worrying about future events, and thinking about and perhaps regretting past events.

Mindfulness is the antidote to mindlessness. It enhances our awareness and teaches us to be in the moment and focus on our present experience. Through guided meditations and other exercises, we can learn to observe our experience with curiosity and accept it without judgment.[5] Practicing mindfulness can be a powerful tool for reducing stress and improving our well-being.

We all experience unpleasant emotions and negative thoughts from time to time. This, according to mindfulness experts, is simply what minds do. Accepting this simple notion enables us to develop a different relationship to negative thoughts and feelings. Rather than believing them or trying to change them, we can observe and accept them. By accepting them as events that come and go, we can put some distance between ourselves and our mental experiences.

Focus on Your Breath   Various forms of mindfulness meditation use the breath as a focal point. By training our mind to focus on our breath, we learn to pay attention to what our experience is right now. When our mind wonders, as it will, we can bring it back to our breath.

Do this exercise at a time and a place where you're on your own and will not be interrupted.

Sit down in a comfortable position. Close your eyes if you're comfortable doing that. Now focus your attention on your breath as it enters your body and leaves your body. Feel the sensation in your belly as it fills with air and then as it deflates when the breath leaves your body. Focus on the breath coming in and on the breath going out. Do this quietly now as you sit here.

Pretty soon, you will find that your mind is no longer on your breath. When you find yourself daydreaming, planning or playing a certain event in your head, just bring your attention back to your breathing. Don't judge yourself or give yourself a hard time. Simply guide your attention back to your breathing. Your attention will wander many times, and you can bring it back whenever you notice this. When you're ready, open your eyes.

When it comes to various domains of life such as interpersonal, community, occupational, physical, psychological, and economic, you can choose to become more mindful. Table 2.1 shows different choices that can make life more mindful or mindless.

Dig a Little Deeper

If you find yourself misaligned, or if you are leading a mindless existence, it may be helpful to dig deeper into your past. Sigmund Freud helped us understand that many of our self-defeating behaviors derive from unconscious motives and unresolved conflicts. Some of these conflicts are with other people, but some are internal. We fight with ourselves.[6] As a result of "unfinished business" we tend to act in ways that are not helpful, to ourselves, or others.

For example, past experiences of betrayal may lead us to distrust coworkers or romantic partners. Previous experiences of failure may prevent us from applying for a new job. A history of aggression within your own family of origin may have taught you that it is OK to act violently to resolve disputes. Alternatively, you may have become so averse to conflict that you let others disrespect you.

Freud thought that some of these experiences are so painful that instead of dealing with them consciously we bury them in the unconscious. The feelings and thoughts associated with negative interactions do not vanish. Instead, they inhabit our unconscious and come out from time to time in uncontrolled ways.

The theory behind this is that some traumatic experiences are so psychologically painful that instead of feeling the pain we suppress and repress the negative feelings and vanish them to the unconscious. The problem is that these painful memories do not go quietly into the unconscious. They may be dormant for a while, but from time to time they appear in ways that are not helpful.

Table 2.1. Mindful and mindless living

	Mindful living	Mindless living
Interpersonal	• Treating people with respect • Being a good listener • Trying to see things from another person's perspective	• Yelling at your partner • Talking about yourself all the time • Being unaware of how you come across
Community	• Thinking about how to improve your community • Volunteering in the community • Taking up a cause that is important to you	• Not bothering to vote • Being indifferent to people in your community • Ignoring community problems
Occupational	• Giving everyone a voice at work • Trying to align your work with your passions and values • Letting workers do what they're best at and enjoy	• Being physically present but psychologically absent • Mindlessly going from one task to the next • Getting distracted without realizing it
Physical	• Clearing junk food from your house • Putting your running shoes by your bed to remind you to exercise in the morning • Putting a plate of cut up fresh veggies in the fridge for a snack	• Eating a bag of chips because it's there • Seeing a commercial for chocolate bars and then getting a chocolate bar from the cupboard • Not exercising because none of your friends do it
Psychological	• Thinking about your values • Seeing yourself as a worthy individual • Being in the moment • Embracing a growth mindset • Understanding your strengths	• Ruminating about an argument you had with your partner • Believing your negative self-talk • Negatively comparing yourself to others
Economic	• Being thoughtful about how you spend your money • Saving for retirement • Thinking about your long-term financial goals	• Buying something on impulse • Spending more because you downloaded an app that makes it even easier to shop • Spending without planning for the future

Based on a history of parental rejection or neglect, you tend to distrust people who really care for you and love you. If your friend forgets to call you at the agreed upon time you think that she no longer cares for you. If you detect the slightest disagreement from a colleague, you react aggressively. In all these instances the unconscious is trying to "protect" you from further pain. The problem is that these protective strategies can be ultimately self-defeating.

Psychoanalysts think that we should be aware of how these defense mechanisms and unconscious dynamics dictate our behavior. According to them, it is useful to know what is going on in our unconscious. The more we know about ourselves and our subterranean dynamics, the more aligned we can be with our goals and our values.

These dynamics affect all of us, but in varying degrees. For some, they just appear in dreams in the form of fears and fantasies. For the most part, they are helpful coping mechanisms. For others, it is a source of concern. If you are experiencing phobias, too much conflict, or relationship problems that persist, it may be worth your while to dig deeper into your history to try to understand how the present may be connected to your past.[7]

All of us have memories we would rather erase, but our mind does not easily let go. Our unconscious is a huge container of memories good and bad. It is often threatening to open the door to the unconscious to see what monsters may be lurking there. There may be painful memories and histories of rejection and shame, but ultimately, it is better to try to control these monsters instead of being controlled by them.

Without some introspection it is difficult to make connections between the past and the present. However, the problem with introspection is that often we are not aware of what we are not aware. In other words, we don't know what we don't know, so we are at a loss as to what to look for. With help from others, such as a partner or a therapist, we can identify our own blind spots. These are behaviors that are known and visible to others, but are not known to us.[8] In other words, we are unaware of them. Other people may see that when we are confronted by colleagues we react sarcastically or aggressively. We may see nothing wrong with it, but others can tell that we are hurting people. This is an example of a behavior that is visible to others but invisible to us.

To help us in our journey of self-awareness, psychoanalysts identified a series of defense mechanisms that help us manage in the short term, but are not always helpful in the long term.[9] One way to know ourselves better is through an analysis of defense mechanisms. These are psychological processes meant to protect us from emotional pain. On the surface, it is good to prevent pain. But if these defense mechanisms prevent us also from getting to the root cause of our problems, they are not very good.[10] We can share with you some of the most common defense mechanisms:

1. *Denial*: This is the refusal to admit that there is a problem affecting you or those around you. People with addictions often deny they have a problem. They bury their head in the sand and pretend that everything is fine. In the meantime, they ruin their lives, incur huge debts, and cause a great deal of pain to their loved ones. We see this often in the case of functioning alcoholics, who manage to work, but are destroying their families.

2. *Repression*: The memory of a negative experience can be so painful that we tend to suppress it or forget it altogether. In my case (Isaac), there are big chunks of my childhood that I do not remember. Both of my parents died in a car accident when I had just turned eight, and the tragedy was so painful that I erased a lot of memories associated with them. Other people who go through severe trauma, such as child abuse, tend to repress these incidents. To some extent, repression is a helpful mechanism because it affords people a chance to function and to cope in light of very stressful events, but in the long run, it is important to deal with these issues lest they cause damage and prevent the individual from flourishing.

3. *Regression*: When faced with real or perceived threats, some people yearn for dependency and the security of a parental figure. Instead of coping with life events, they want somebody to take over for them and make it "all go away," as when they were children. Another sign of regression is trying to solve problems through fights instead of dialogue. In this case regression means forgetting to put the break on certain impulses like swearing or acting violently. With time, we are all expected to engage in self-regulation. Regression does away with all that. In many cases, people regress when under stress and recover to adult functioning when the stressors are removed.

4. *Displacement*: We often direct aggression toward something or someone who is not threatening. So, instead of being upset with your boss because he is a jerk and makes you stay late, you come home frustrated and direct your anger toward your children or the dog, whomever you see first! In essence, displacement is the redirecting of feelings or behaviors toward an object or person who is not as threatening as the source of

discomfort. You can feel pretty safe arguing with your husband, but pretty unsafe challenging your boss. As a result, the frustration that your boss caused is channeled toward your loved ones instead.

5. *Projection*: In this mechanism you attribute to other people unpleasant motives that you harbor yourself. If you feel envious or jealous you project that negative attribute to others and say how "jealous" they are. Similarly, if you covet wealth but are unwilling to admit it, you deride others for being so obsessed with material possessions.

6. *Intellectualization*: Instead of dealing with the emotional consequences of a painful event, such as a separation, you philosophize about the importance of independence and self-determination. Engaging in intellectual discourse prevents you from dealing with feelings of sadness and depression. As with all defense mechanisms, a moderate use of them may be beneficial to the person in question. No one knows for sure when a person is ready to confront sadness. Therefore, it is vital to acknowledge the salutary, if temporary aspects of defense mechanisms. At some point, however, it is healthy to confront the pain to prevent it from playing tricks with you, such as stopping you from engaging in new relationships.

7. *Rationalization*: Similar to intellectualization, this defense mechanism involves cognitive gymnastics to pretend that an event is not really painful or your fault. If your girlfriend dumps you, it is easier to say that she was not good anyway than to admit that you are hurting. Rationalizing is about making excuses for undesirable behaviors or problems. If you fail to meet a deadline at work, you find plenty of people to blame instead of taking responsibility for your behavior.

8. *Undoing*: Following a mistake, you try to compensate or overcompensate by engaging in counteracting behavior. If you offend a loved one, you may shower praise on her in the hope that the new behavior will compensate for the previous one.

9. *Sublimation*: This is the channeling of socially inappropriate thoughts or feelings into more appropriate ones. This is by far one of the most adaptive defense mechanisms. Instead of acting on hostile impulses toward a person or an institution, you can make a joke instead. For some people sports is an acceptable way to get rid of excess testosterone.

10. *Reaction formation*: This is doing the opposite of what one feels or thinks because the feelings or thoughts are socially unacceptable. Someone who is prejudiced against a person may be exceedingly solicitous toward her just to hide his true feelings.

What defense mechanisms have in common is the covering of unacceptable thoughts, feelings, or behaviors, and their transformation into more acceptable ways of expressing oneself and coping.[11] To some extent, they are all adaptive.[12] But overuse may lead to dysfunction, as the user remains unaware of her motives.[13] At some point, all these defenses prevent us from being authentic and from flourishing.

Remember, one of the side effects of defense mechanisms is to maintain the status quo. If your status quo is not satisfactory, observing your defense mechanisms may help you shake things up. This is the essence of self-awareness. To know yourself is to understand not just your values and goals but also your unconscious motives.

Admittedly, this is not something most people do on a regular basis. To begin with, we are not taught to self-reflect. In addition, this type of self-reflection requires skills. The ability to know yourself is predicated on the fact that you know how to do it. You can go to a therapist, and many people certainly benefit from that, but you can also become your own detective.

Self-awareness is essentially about making connections. If you try to link events of the past with the present, what you dream at night with what fear during the day, and interactions with recurring frustrations, you may see patterns the way a detective sees patterns in a crime scene. It is all about seeing how certain parts of your life connect to others. Behaviors are linked to emotions and thoughts in a continual loop.

Set a SMART Goal

To know yourself better, and to play detective, you can start by setting a goal. If you find yourself in trouble or are just plain frustrated, you can *set a goal* to look inward. You can set a goal to review your feelings, thoughts, and behaviors once a week. You can select a day of the week, like Sunday, to review how you felt the preceding week. Have you argued too much with your spouse? Have you experienced satisfaction at work?

Reviewing your week is a SMART goal: *specific, measurable, achievable, relevant,* and *time limited.* It is very specific in that you can review your feelings, thoughts, and actions. It is measurable because you can do it once a week for four weeks. It is also achievable because it is not too hard and it is relevant to your life and time limited.

If you find yourself using too many defense mechanisms such as displacement, projection, or undoing, you may want to ask yourself where the need for these comes from. If you find that you are not completely truthful to your spouse, boss, and even to yourself, you better pay attention to that.

You can also use the technique we call *write a new story.* You may have a story that says "I'm fine with the way I am and I don't need any kind of introspection." A lot of males certainly behave that way. Furthermore, you may have this story reinforced by your friends, who encourage you not to "overthink" things too much. You may live by a story that says "my problems are the result of the idiots around me; I'm just fine." You can begin creating a new story by asking yourself if this story is really serving you well.

You can also *read cues* to understand what situations trigger frustration and which ones make you happy. You can also challenge negative assumptions such as *thinking in polarizing* and *all or none terms.* Dividing the world into wonderful and terrible people is an example of all or none thinking. Another cognitive error is thinking that if you fail at one thing you are a complete failure. We call this *generalizing.*

All these activities amount to a personal checkup. Just like you take your car to the mechanic for a tune up and an oil change once in a while, you need to take yourself to the self-reflection garage once in a while. Your emotional life deserves no less than your car. If you have been listening to your doctor, you go for a physical once a year. You can do something similar with your psychological well-being. You can do it yourself, or you can go to a professional, but it is good practice to stop and evaluate where is your life going from time to time.

The answer may be that you are feeling fulfilled, happy, and satisfied with your relationship, work, and hobbies. But if the answer is less than favorable, you can do a self-checkup. It is hard to self-reflect when you are in the middle of an argument or are stressed out due to deadlines. Nevertheless, self-reflection can prevent future problems and enhance your well-being.

You can engage in weekly self-reflection: you can go to a professional for a psychological checkup, or you can ask a friend to share with you how she sees you. As noted earlier, we all have certain blind spots. These are things other people see in us, but we do not see in ourselves. A trusted friend or relative can share with you these useful impressions. Asking for help is a great first step. Sometimes talking to a friend can help you discern complicated stuff, but beware of advice. Make sure your friend is listening to you and not to his own inner voice. Beware of friends who want you to pursue their dreams and not yours. It is difficult enough sometimes to figure out what we want for ourselves. We certainly don't need others confusing us with their projections.

Your weekly checkup can be a good time to ask yourself if your current goals are self-concordant or not. Are you pursuing a job that really meets your needs or are you just doing it because your parents insisted that you become a lawyer, doctor, or investment banker? To pursue a self-concordant goal, one that you enjoy and find meaningful, requires courage. You need courage to challenge convention and sometimes go against the grain. You may find late in life that your calling is in the arts and not in accounting. It is certainly hard to switch careers, but it is even harder to stick with something you don't find meaningful or enjoyable.

Socrates is quoted as saying that *the unexamined life is not worth living.* Socrates paid a heavy price for questioning the status quo in Athens. Leaders did not take kindly to his challenge of convention. Fortunately, you don't have to pay such heavy price. Knowing your values and aspirations on one hand and your unconscious motives on the other can shine a light on your life. Once you are self-aware, you can look at issues with a critical eye.

Know the Issue

To improve your wellness, you must be well informed and aware of your biases and defense mechanisms. Spend a little time exploring the issue you want to tackle, as well as your own preconceptions.

There are a lot of myths out there. Years ago, doctors believed that smoking was not bad for you. So much for that one! Today you'd be hard-pressed to find anyone who doesn't know that smoking is dangerous to your health. However, it's not always obvious what is accurate and what is not.

If you want to improve your wellness you must inform yourself. You need to be able to distinguish myth from reality so that you make decisions based on credible information. Most of us use Google or some other search engine as the initial starting point. While Google is an excellent way of gathering information about a topic, not all websites are equally credible. You have to be an informed consumer. So be sure to check your sources!

Knowing how to search for information is important, but unfortunately, people are resistant to information that is inconsistent with their beliefs or behavior. Someone who loves his daily doughnut may not want to hear about the perils of trans-fats or processed sugar. A student who procrastinates may be uncomfortable learning that studying in small chunks is much better than trying to cram it all in at the end. And a serial spender may have all kinds of reasons why credit card debt is not a problem.

Resistance to information is often an indication that someone is not ready to make a change in his or her life. For now, consider the possibility that you may resist information not because it is false but because it makes you uncomfortable. If you truly want to improve your well-being, you have to be open to learning about the behavior you want to change.

At times, sticking your head in the sand can come with a heavy price tag. Ignoring overdue bills can cause financial damage, while ignoring your doctor's warning about unhealthy eating can lead to physical damage.

When presented with information that is inconsistent with our plans, most of us experience discomfort. Table 2.2 shows some examples of

- Common behaviors that people engage in
- Information that may contradict the behaviors
- Excuses people use to deal with the discomfort created by the information
- A possible strategy to deal with the new information

Look at the examples and then come up with some that pertain to your own life and goals in the blank cells.

If you're honest with yourself, you would have discovered in the exercise that you tend to ignore information that contradicts your behavior. No point feeling guilty about this though. The best thing you can do is to set a goal related to the information obtained. If you want to drink more water, set a goal of increasing consumption by one more glass per day.

You can then *create a positive habit* by putting a refillable bottle on your desk. You can also *challenge negative assumptions* about yourself, such as "I will never change" or "the damage has already been done to my lungs." As we shall see later in the book, you can *introduce into your environment positive cues,* such as water bottles, and *eliminate negative cues,* such as removing the candy bowl from your desk.

Time for comic relief. You have been learning about serious stuff for a while now. Let's see if you can laugh yourself to heightened awareness in the next section.

THE LAUGHING SIDE

So much to be aware of! First, you have to be aware of your own habits. You have to become your own detective. Second, you must be knowledgeable about the issue that is affecting your health and wellness. This is too much!

To succeed in raising awareness of your own habits, pretend you carry a mirror and everything you do is the subject of reflection. It is amazing what you will discover. You will realize—my favorite—that you and 99 percent of the people you know do not use a knife to push food toward the fork. Instead, you will see that you push food toward your fork with *your fingers.* This is the most disgusting habit ever. Hello! This is what knives are for. You do not put your fingers in your plate. No need to bring germs into your spinach. Ironically, these are the same people who carry with them bottles of hand sanitizers wherever they go.

Table 2.2.   How to Overcome Excuses to Act on Useful Information

My behavior	Information that contradicts my behavior	My excuse	Strategies to deal with new information
Example: I eat too many chocolate bars, doughnuts, and candy.	Example: Eating too many sweets is not healthy.	Example: "It won't kill me."	Example: I will learn more about the risk of becoming prediabetic. I will start cutting down slowly and gradually.
Example: I barely drink two glasses of water a day.	Example: You need to drink at least eight glasses of water a day.	Example: "I drink lots of coffee instead."	Example: I will make sure to have a refillable water bottle next to my desk.
Example: I've been smoking since I was sixteen years of age	Example: Cigarettes are extremely dangerous to your health	Example: "I tried quitting before and it hasn't worked. No point trying again."	Example: I will implement proven strategies such as setting achievable goals, creating positive habits, finding alternatives, and asking for support.
Your Turn:			
Your Turn:			
Your Turn:			

Just look around. You will be amazed at the frequency with which people use their fingers to shovel food onto their forks. *Please stop this madness!*

The second component of awareness involves learning about the subject matter itself. If you want to lower your blood pressure, you learn something about it. If you want to reduce stress, you read up on it. If you want to prevent venereal diseases, you stay home. If you're like most human beings, you'll get your facts from fact-checked, solid, and reliable sources, such as *60 Minutes*. Oh, no, wait a minute. Breaking news just arrived on our desk. It turns out that Lara Logan from *60 Minutes* recently broadcast an interview full of fabrications. The *60 Minutes* reporter interviewed a guy who made up a fantastic story about the Benghazi attack on the US embassy. Besides, Lara Logan also pushes food onto her fork with her fingers. So forget *60 Minutes* and try some other authoritative sources, such as Fox News, or theonion.com. Both of these outlets have similar reliability ratings.

Alternatively, you can turn to Brian Williams from NBC, who took a leave of absence after an episode of self-aggrandizement. Mr. Williams reported that he was in a helicopter hit by enemy fire in Iraq. It turned out that too many veterans were there to disprove his claim. After a public apology, he went on leave. If all fails, you can turn to Donald Trump for reliable, predictable, honest, and consistent lunacy.

Some other basic rules apply when you want to learn about a topic. Call me paranoid, but check the funding source. If doctors are pushing certain medications and getting personal benefits from the pharmaceutical companies, think twice before you follow their advice. In the 1950s, doctors used to recommend Camel cigarettes, which I'm sure had all kinds of medicinal properties. The problem is that these medicinal properties killed you.

The following stories pertain, mostly, to the comic side of being clueless. Lack of personal and social awareness usually brings a smile. The stories show how people are either unaware of themselves or blissfully ignorant of their surroundings.

Patriotism

Recently, Moldova won the distinction of having the highest rate of alcohol consumption in the world by a huge margin, which makes it a favorite destination for college students. A few years earlier, it ranked last in the world in terms of life satisfaction, which makes it a preferred destination for suicidal people. It is also the poorest country in Europe, attracting many destitute people who want to feel in good company.

In 2008, Eric Weiner documented in *The Geography of Bliss* the utter desperation most people experience there, which makes it a Mecca for existential writers. Finally, a couple of years ago, Transparency International wrote a scathing report about the level of corruption in Moldova, which makes it an excellent training ground for Miami politicians. There are a lot of cues and reasons why moving to Moldova may not be a good idea, despite my yearning to be in touch with my roots.

For the past fifty-eight years, I have managed to hide the fact that my ancestors were from Moldova. When people detect an accent, I tell them that I was born in Argentina and lived in several places, like Nashville, which have influenced the inflection of my voice. My parents were also born in Argentina; so technically I'm not lying by hiding my Moldovan roots.

I managed to keep my Moldovan secret for years until I found myself in a restaurant with friends in Boca Raton a few months ago. My friend asked the cheerful waitress where she was from, and the next thing I know I'm telling her that my ancestors were also from Moldova.

Irina (not her real name; her real name was Ioana) told us that she came to the United States from Moldova a few years ago. She was ecstatic to hear that my grandparents were from her country and proceeded to share with us the Encyclopedia Britannica version of

Moldova's history. For twenty-four minutes, she stood next to us and gushed about the many atrocities that were bestowed upon her countrymen and women since the establishment of the Principality of Moldavia in 1359.

As a former history teacher in Moldova, she was obviously starved for an audience, while I was starved for lunch. While she was getting hotter and hotter with the telling of every invasion by Crimean Tatars, my entrée was getting colder and colder. She was totally clueless about the cues that we were there to eat, and not get a lecture. Irina got so involved in the telling that she was completely oblivious of some very prominent contextual cues: waitress, guests, menu, food, hunger. She was totally unaware of our hopes for some lunch.

When she got to the Treaty of Bucharest in 1812, I decided to start eating between calamities. Unless I started eating, I was going to become the next victim of the Russian Empire, which annexed Moldova and gave it the name Oblast of Moldavia and Bessarabia. When Oblast was converted to the Bessarabia Governorate in 1871, I decided the hell with it and attacked my food with the same vigor that Romania went after Bukovina and Transylvania.

When she got to the beginning of last century, Irina went back to get us desserts. I used the opportunity to finish my plate and recover from the carnage. After serving dessert, Irina went straight to Bessarabia's proclamation of Independence from Russia on February 6, 1918, conveniently skipping the first eighteen years of the century, at which point I asked her about the Kishinev pogrom of 1903 in which dozens of Jews were murdered and hundreds wounded.

It turned out that our adorable hostess was never taught the incident that prompted the exile of my ancestors. When she started squirming, I asked her about the second pogrom that took place between October 19 and 20 of 1905. At that point, she told us that she needed to serve other customers, to which I asked if she knew of the Jewish community in Kalarash, just outside Kishinev, which is where my ancestors were from. While I was relishing my revenge, unbeknownst to me, I gave her more ammunition. Kalarash, she told us, is where the best cognac in the world is distilled. She went on and on about the cognac. At that point, I gave up on ordering dessert because I would have been late for my next appointment, which brings me to the big lesson of the day: If I had kept my mouth shut about Moldova, as I have for the last fifty-eight years, I could have eaten a hot lunch and enjoyed a nice dessert.

The Chutzpah Diaries: An Anti-Autobiography

Preface

I'm allergic to arrogance and am disdainful of people who are unaware of their pomposity. If I ever engage in either, please wave a red flag in front of me.

Introduction

Here goes my premise: If you have the chutzpah to write about yourself, then you should only write about chutzpah, because that is the only thing for which you can claim any sort of expertise. The alternatives are that you're either arrogant or unaware of your pomposity. The only other option is that you're running for office, in which case we can expect multiple biographies from you until you get elected or die, whichever comes first.

Chapter 1: Prenatal Chutzpah

My first memorable act of chutzpah was competing against 300 million sperm to fertilize an egg, and winning. I'm not making this up. It's a fact. I looked it up on YouTube. Before I watched the cute animation, I used to think that I competed with, like, 20 sperm; but 300 million? That's chutzpah! I only wish I had been a sperm with smaller ears and manly voice, but what can you do. I'm sure I got a girly voice because of all the screaming that went on in the fallopian tube while other sperm were pulling at my ears to stop me. Come to think of it, my voice and ears are not sources of shame; they're war wounds.

Chapter 2: Pubescent Chutzpah

My second act of chutzpah was finishing high school. For most of my teenage years I had three clear priorities: my girlfriend, soccer, and the youth movement. I attended—physically but not mentally—a Hebrew day school in Argentina on a scholarship. For several years, since my parents died when I was eight years old, the Jewish community provided scholarships so that my siblings and I could remain in the private school. That was very nice of them. I should have been more gracious and studied more, but priorities are priorities, especially for teenagers.

In grade 9, I failed math and Spanish! I probably forgot to hand in assignments. Failing a course during the regular academic year meant that you had to study for an exam during the summer. So study I did, and I actually enjoyed it, but it was not until I moved to Israel in grade 11 that I really discovered the love of learning. In Israel, the youth movement disappeared, my girlfriend and I went our separate ways, and soccer in the Middle East was nothing to write home about, so I found myself unencumbered by old passions and nurtured a new one: learning. But most importantly, I had the chutzpah to finish at the top of my class, even in Math!

Chapter 3: Adolescent Chutzpah

Leaving for Israel involved some chutzpah as well. Being part of a youth movement that opposed the fascist dictatorship in Córdoba, Argentina, was dangerous. So at the age of fifteen, I called a meeting of the "senior" leadership of the movement, which in effect consisted of four people: my girlfriend, a sixteen-year-old boy, his girlfriend, and I. The average age of the "senior" leadership team was fourteen years and eight months. We spent one entire night thinking about what to do with a youth movement of about 150 kids.

If we continued with our activities, we would have endangered our members, who were actively opposing the military dictatorship, and that was no joke. If we merged with another Jewish youth movement, which was an option, we would have given up on our belief system because the other organization was not as "idealist" as we were. So the "senior" leaders of the movement decided to pack up and move to Israel. We were about to make Aliyah. We had the nerve to tell a group of parents that we wanted to leave and take their kids with us. Needless to say, some parents thought we were crazy, but some were very supportive, only reinforcing our Chutzpah.

Chapter 4: Occupational Chutzpah

When I finished boarding school, I needed to support myself. One of my teachers got me a job cleaning houses in Ramat Aviv, a nice Tel Aviv neighborhood. Most apartments in Israel have famous plastic shutters called *treessim*, and cleaning them is a craft I had not yet mastered. Apparently you had to have been born in Israel to understand their inner workings. My short time in boarding school had not prepared me for the challenge, but I needed a job, and when asked if I knew how to clean *treessim*, I said, "Of course."

I introduced myself politely to the lady of the house, who commented on my cute Argentinean accent. She also praised my Hebrew. I was glowing with pride. We talked for a few minutes about Zvi Yampolski (the teacher who had introduced us), exchanged a few pleasantries, and off I went to clean while she went to work.

Vacuuming was a piece of cake, doing dishes was fine, but shutters, that was something else. I did not have the faintest idea how to clean them. I remember smudging dirt all over them. Despite my best efforts, I was unable to remove the cake of mud that I had managed to build in remote places that I couldn't reach for a second time. To clean the mess that I had created, I would have had to risk my life by climbing on top of the railing, which I had no intention of doing. They never called me back. I felt really bad for the family, and for Zvi. To make a living, I switched to waiting tables, working the night shift as a guard at the student dorm, and teaching part time at a rehab center for youth with intellectual disabilities.

Chapter 5: Masterly Chutzpah

I did OK during my undergrad studies, but I was not a stellar student. No sooner had I mastered Hebrew than I had to learn all the course materials in English; my third language. That was a trying period. Two new languages in two years was a lot to deal with. I really doubted that I would get into a master's program in psychology. My grades were decent, but to get into one of the clinical programs in the very few universities around the country, you had to excel, which I did not.

I somehow got an interview for the child clinical psychology program at Tel Aviv University. I had a series of individual and group interviews, and don't ask me how, but I got in. I was the youngest applicant to the program and my grades were not superb, but I insisted that I had something to offer. I got into the program by sheer chutzpah. The only other alternative was that I was very charming, but I'm not going there because some readers with a lack of appreciation for metaphor will shoot me.

Chapter 5: The Mother of all Chutzpah

During the second year of my master's program I had to do some field work. Twenty-two years of age, I chose none other than to run a parenting group. While most of the parents in the group were polite and understanding of the fact that I was only a student, there was one mother who made minced meat of me. She flatly told me that I could not run a parenting group if I did not have children.

No amount of psychological training had prepared me for her belligerence. She probably thought that I was the one who needed some parenting, and she did not hesitate to tell me how to run the group and when to change my underwear. While I was coping with her frontal assault, I could not help notice that she was accompanied by a beautiful young woman. Had it not been for the chutzpah to run a parenting group, I would have missed the opportunity to meet the striking young woman who eventually became my wife!

Chapter 5: Doctoral Chutzpah

For my PhD at the University of Manitoba in Canada, I decided to challenge convention. Instead of basing my dissertation on an empirical study, which usually involved torturing rats in two different ways, measuring the magnitude of their convulsions, and running some stats on them, I decided to write a philosophical critique of psychology. It turned out that abandoning the standard of an empirical study was sacrilege. I really didn't mean to raise the ire of my professors, but I caused a small revolution in the department.

How dare I, a PhD student with a heavy accent, challenge the very profession that was about to bestow on me a doctorate? The thing is, I'm a very congenial person and had meant no disrespect, but the reaction from some professors was vengeful. Some of them tried to fail me while others wanted me to change the topic of my dissertation.

With the support of my dissertation committee chair, Freddy Marcuse, I plowed ahead and managed to put together a committee that consisted of no less than six professors, including a philosopher and a professor of English who specialized in literary criticism. All along I was told that the dissertation must be of publishable quality. That was drilled into me time and again. I had been challenged.

While jumping the million hoops that the department of psychology erected for me, I decided to write a summary of my dissertation and send it to one of the most highly respected journals in psychology. Two days before the dissertation defense—the Day of Judgment where professors crucify you with questions they don't have an answer for—a summary of my thesis was published in the *American Psychologist*, the flagship journal of the American Psychological Association. My supervisor walked into the defense with my paper in hand, showing it off proudly to the other professors the way a father shows off his newborn baby.

The knockout came from the letter of the external examiner. My dissertation had been sent to George Albee, former president of the American Psychological Association, for review and approval. Albee sent back a glowing report. That paper in the *American Psychologist* launched my academic career and opened many doors for me. Chutzpah saved me. Without the gumption to challenge the stuffiness of the psych department, my career would have looked much different today. Had I listened to my professors, now I would have been inducing convulsions in albino rats.

Pet-Friendly Florida

Florida is the most inclusive state in the nation. The Sunshine State welcomes not just people from all over but also species that you've only encountered in nightmares, like termites, bats, snakes, and reptiles. If you want to live here, you need to know what you're getting into, though I, Isaac, have proof that the people of Florida are friendly to all these animals and insects. Take termites for example. After I signed the contract with the University of Miami, they broke the news to me: *everybody* has termites in South Florida.

We promptly hired a reputable pest control company whose employees wore very nice uniforms and whose schedule was totally unpredictable. So friendly was this company to termites that for several years they totally ignored the fact that they had eaten five feet of fascia over our garage.

Needless to say, up until that day I had no idea what fascia was, in any language. As I was trying to explain the situation over the phone to the pest control company, they kept throwing at me words like *sheathing, soffit, rafters, truss, underlayment, fascia,* and *dormer,* which made me feel like an idiot. Several google trips later, I was able to confirm that it was the *fascia* that had been eaten. Do people learn these words in school? Do they take roofing 101 in Florida? Do they learn about termites in kindergarten?

When I confronted the neatly uniformed, bilingual pest control general, he said that termites don't do that kind of damage. They were still covering up for the insects. At that point, I called two more pest control companies, and Manolo, my friend the builder. No question about it, unanimous judgment: termites.

To make sure that no opportunity goes wasted, we decided to fire the pest control company and go instead with a "green" provider. The latter explained to us that it's all organic and environmentally friendly. So friendly was their treatment of pests that for several months we saw an increase in the number of roaches munching on our fruit overnight. When I politely asked our green supplier if roaches can get used to their treatment, he said that they change the product every time to prevent inoculation. OK, I got it. January was vanilla, February was citrus, and March was honeysuckle flavor. Our roaches couldn't be happier.

In an effort to be supportive, Ora, my wife, had suggested that perhaps it was rodents and not cockroaches that had been eating our fruit. Our cleaning lady concurred, motivating me to sell the house and move to Alberta, which has been rodent-free for fifty years. I did do my homework.

I consulted again with our green pest control guy, who said there was a definitive way to determine the culprit: poop. Cockroach poop has a vertical edge; rat poop ends diagonally. He went on and on about sphincter anatomy in rodents and insects and the evolutionary causes of their differences.

Just when I thought that I knew way too much about insects in Florida, I had to take a magnifying glass to examine their shit. I wanted to prove to Ora, and Isis, our cleaning lady, that there were no rodents in my house.

Sure enough, the poop, which was all over our fruit plate, had a distinct vertical edge, which proved beyond reasonable doubt that we had plenty of roaches. As if that wasn't strong enough evidence, I picked up a grapefruit from the plate and out came crawling, from a hole the size of an igloo, a giant cockroach.

If there is anything I hate more than rats, it's big rats, which is what possums are. Possums feel at home in Coral Gables. They roam around like they own the place. So it came as no surprise when we discovered a couple of them nesting in our backyard. Next to our useless swimming pool (too small to swim in, too cold to get close to), we have a very expensive motor that cleans the water we never swim in, as well as a device that operates an amphibious vacuum cleaner that consumes more energy than the country of Benin.

The motors are encased in a structure covered by a piece of plywood. Whenever the submersible hoover gets stuck, I muck around with the motor and pretend to know what the heck I'm doing. Imagine my surprise when I discovered not one but two possums relaxing next to the motors. They had brought leafs and sticks to make their own Sealy Posturepedic. They had apparently lifted the wood cover and managed to return it to its place, just to shock me.

Ora and I debated what to do. We were really ambivalent about the whole thing. We felt for the creatures. After all, we're vegan; believe in interspecies justice and all that mushy stuff. But I really dislike these animals. They revolt me. So we decided to do nothing.

A few days later I went to visit our lodgers and found them in Kama Sutra pose number sixty-nine. They were totally oblivious to my inspection, showing great sexual dexterity, and @#&$ (rhymes with tucking) their brains out. This went on for a few days. In addition to revulsion, now I had reason to feel voyeuristic guilt.

Mr. and Mrs. Possum occupied our pool motor home for a few more days until we saw them leaving their abode to forage for food. I reluctantly removed their possessions and secured the wood cover with several bricks. It was heartbreaking to see them return to find out that they had been evicted. We wanted to compensate them with some oxycodone and Viagra pills, but they would have none of it. We saw them leaving, carrying their Kama Sutra guide on their backs. They were obviously offended.

Our backyard is not just friendly to quadrupedal diprotodon marsupials, but also to all kinds of bugs and birds that enjoy mango for dessert. To feel Floridians, we planted a few trees as soon as we bought the house. Watching our mango tree grow has been especially rewarding. Sharing it with white flies and the entire ornithological kingdom has not.

Ora watches our mangos like a hawk herself. The problem is that she reminds me in the middle of the night to go and fetch the mangos that might have ripened since I squished them three hours ago. "Isaac, I hear birds near our mango tree; don't just lie there, do something." "Don't worry, Ora, I'm sure it's the possums trying the latest marsupial Kama Sutra."

I have a trauma with bird poop, which is why I hesitate to get near them while they hover over our mangos. When my nephew Gabi was seven years old, he flew by himself from Israel to Winnipeg to visit us. We wanted him to have a good time so I took him to the Zoo in Assiniboine Park. Being Winnipeg, the choices were polar bears, mosquitoes, or imported birds from the tropics. The giant cage with multicolor birds looked really interesting.

As soon as we entered the sanctuary, a bird managed to drop its shit exactly between the rim of my sunglasses and my eyebrows, making a perfect landing on my right eye. My trauma was worth Gabi's laughter. I had never seen anybody laugh so hard. When Gabi finally calmed down, I asked him to remove the shit from my eye, which resulted in further smudging of poop all over my face and a second bout of explosive laughter. Since then, I cannot look at birds without an umbrella.

I survived the termites, the roaches, the possums, and even Ora's commands in the middle of the night, but I nearly collapsed when I discovered the black snake in our bathroom. Imagine this. We're new to South Florida, I go pee, and without any warning, a black snake slithers from behind the toilet. I did then what every self-respecting male would do: I shut the door, ran to the phone, and called my neighbor. Trying to sound less panicky than I really was, I rung Stewart. He grew up in Florida, so he would surely know what do. "Don't worry, Dean, it must be a garden snake. I'll be right over." Stewart calls me Dean because we both work at the University of Miami, and he is very deferential; very nice of him. Nicer yet was the fact that he came over with a flashlight and some garden gloves.

I was so relieved to see him. I'm sure this is how people in occupied Europe felt when they saw the US army. Stewart was our knight in a shining armor. Of course by the time he came the snake had disappeared into a hole right behind our toilet, where some pipes connect the tank to the Everglades. I still have no idea what these pipes do, other than provide a conduit for snakes that come from the Everglades to Miami to reclaim their territory.

I avoided that bathroom for weeks. I had images of a snake coming out of the toilet bowl, swimming upstream, just as I was about to clean my rear end. But soon enough it emerged from the crevice behind the toilet bowl; and in a surge of testosterone I trapped it between a broom and a shovel and threw it out to the garden. That was the most heroic thing I ever did. Forget fighting the dictatorship in Argentina, or punching Aldo in the face for throwing a rock at my mom's car when we were six years old. That was my LeBron James moment. But wait, there is more.

On our first walk around campus at the University of Miami, we saw plenty of signs near Lake Osceola warning people about crocodiles in the lake. Initially we thought that the signs were just for liability reasons, for the one in a million case that a croc shows up and eats a philosophy student, but we were quickly disabused of our misconceptions.

Ora, who is prone to spotting whales, sharks, dolphins, and crocodiles in puddles, told me that she saw a crocodile in the lake. Mostly, these are figments of her overactive imagination, but this one could not be easily ignored. We lived right by the lake when we moved to the University of Miami, so this sighting deserved attention. That was no simple roach or possum.

We did not need binoculars. The crocodile was right there, ten feet from our porch. I seized the moment. That was my chance to establish my credibility as a responsible senior administrator at the university. I called security right away and reported the sighting. I told them exactly where we saw it, and they promptly replied that they'll look into it. This exchange with campus security was to be repeated several times in the upcoming days: We see the croc, I freak out, I call in a panic; they tell me they'll look into it. Repeat as needed.

This went on for several weeks until one day it dawned on me that the crocodile had probably been there for decades, and the security folks were having a grand time making fun of me every time I called. "Hey guys, listen to this, it's the Dean with the funny accent again. He wants us to capture the croc." They must have put me on loudspeakers for everyone to laugh. Upon further investigation, it turned out that, indeed, the croc had been there for a long time, and since they're an endangered species nobody can do anything about it unless they dismember a football player.

Ora was thoroughly enchanted with the croc. We called him Shmulik. Ora would go over and work by the lake just to spend time with Shmulik. She would grade papers while babysitting her pet. They bonded. She also took pride in warning clueless students about his presence. Ora must have taken ten thousand pictures of Shmulik in her iPhone. The love affair went on for a couple of years, until a person from another state sneaked into the university at night and decapitated our friend for its skin. How do we know it was not a Floridian? Floridians don't do that kind of thing. Floridians are pet friendly.

Low Expectations

The bitter cold aggravating most of the country was of sufficient schadenfreude value that Ora and I decided to watch the Weather Channel. While we were experiencing our two days of winter here in Miami, with temperatures in the low sixties, we reminisced about our days in Canada when we were young and stupid.

Meanwhile, the host of the Weather Channel invited a veterinarian to comment on the well-being of pets during the stormy weather. Dr. Chow said that all pets are different and that some of them are more tolerant of cold than others. She told viewers that "St. Bernard dogs cope better than Chihuahuas with cold."

That was the moment when it all came together for me. Dr. Chow epitomized all that is wrong with this country: low expectations. If you're going on national TV, don't you want to say something a little smarter? Are you not aware that you're on national TV? Is this all you know about the issue? Dr. Chow showed subzero awareness of the issues or herself for that matter.

I've been on TV to talk about serious stuff only a few times, but every time I went on I studied the topic in great depth. In contrast, my co-panelists invented answers that had zero empirical evidence and absolutely no grounding in research. Like Dr. Chow, they had very low expectations of themselves.

Instead of taking responsibility for their actions, many people blame diseases for their lack of judgment and ethical lapses. Instead of expecting decent behavior from their son, the parents of Ethan Couch hired a psychologist who claimed the teenager had a bad case of "affluenza": the result of rich parents who never set proper limits for the kid. Ethan, for whom his parents had no expectations, killed four people while drinking and driving and got away with only probation.

I came to this country because I thought that personal responsibility was big here. Instead, I found a bunch of low-performing, mediocre politicians, professionals and celebrities ready to blame the world but themselves for their shortcomings. No wonder that the totally politically incorrect Amy Chua is gaining traction.

The author of *Battle Hymn for the Tiger Mother* and *The Triple Package* (with hubby Jed Rubenfeld) claims that success relies on three characteristics: impulse control, feelings of inferiority, and feelings of superiority. I think I'm going to join the Amy Chua movement of sadomasochist believers in high expectations. I already fulfill two of her requirements. In fact, I invented impulse control and feelings of inferiority. I'm working now on feelings of super- iority, but it's not going well. Nobody believes me.

Informed Indecisions

The war on Syria presented the last three presidents with tough decisions. Presidential histo- rians say that most decisions by commanders in chief are a close call, unless you're George W. Bush, who was a self-proclaimed decider, and did not know where Syria was; or your name is Donald Trump, who does not know what a moral dilemma is. President Obama, in turn, was criticized for taking too long to make decisions such as whether to bomb Syria or not.

I understand presidents because I also have tough decisions to make, such as watching *Dancing with the Stars* or reruns of *The Big Bang Theory*; eating in or going out; brown rice or quinoa.

My family and I have moved around quite a bit, and every time we have to buy a house, I have the same urge: to buy the first house the realtor shows us. My discerning wife, on the contrary, likes to see 329 houses before we decide what to buy. When we moved to Miami, I was all set to buy the first condo we saw, until Ora reminded me, and the despondent realtor, that we had 328 to go before we could make a decision.

Ora, my meticulous wife, likes to explore all angles of our decisions. Every airplane ticket we buy must be compared across seventeen internet sites to get the best deal. By the time we compare and contrast, and want to buy the first one we saw, which usually has the best price, the ticket is no longer available. I never thought I would say this, but Ora is more like Obama, and I'm more like GW.

When we moved to Australia from Canada, I operated like GW. I landed in Sydney in May 1999, and after half an hour of landing, I called Ora to tell her that we are moving to Australia, at which point she said that I was crazy. A few months later, we moved to Australia and we looked at 329 houses before we bought the first one we saw.

Meat Eaters Suddenly Go Vegetarian

Awareness is about knowing yourself and knowing the issue. Some people are totally clueless about themselves and their behaviors.

Carnivores, who make up 98 percent of the world population, suddenly realize they are eating animals. It was not until February 2014, when the Copenhagen Zoo killed a giraffe and fed it to the lions, that carnivores made the connection between killing animals and their steak. "Come to think of it, I never made the connection," said Jeff O'Brian from Tuscaloosa. "I want to thank CNN for bringing this to my attention. I'm done eating animals, from now on I'm only eating chicken," he said.

In barbecue picnics around the world, demonstrators protested the killing of Marius the giraffe. "Pass me the bacon," said Theresa Kluless, as she held a placard denouncing the Danish government in Nashville.

In China, students were discussing the horrible tragedy as they were sipping shark fin soup in ivory bowls in Beijing. In Japan, mothers in a park were aghast. "It is unacceptable to kill a cute giraffe and feed it to the lions," said one in Tokyo as she offered her child a dolphin sushi.

Meanwhile, the Beef Association of America published a full-page ad in papers across the country denouncing the killing of Marius. "Giraffes are cute animals. They deserve protection from humans." Similar condemnation came from the Chicken Growers Association: "In

America we treat animals humanly. We would never dream of showing them on TV before we kill them. It is very stressful to the animals."

Of the 6.86 billion meat eaters around the world, 3 promised to become vegetarians in solidarity with Marius. For veggie people, this is very encouraging news. At this rate, it would take only 2.078999 billion years and 3.44521 billion slaughtered giraffes for the entire world to become vegetarian. For others, this whole vegetarian thing is moving way too fast. Cattle growers are afraid that some other zoo in Denmark will by mistake kill a cow on TV and lead three more people to a vegetarian lifestyle.

Diplomatic efforts are under way to remove all cows from Denmark and hide them in an undisclosed location. Our sources tell us that it will be either Guantanamo or the new Trump Golf Course in Doral. "Both places have plenty of grass," said our contact in condition of anonymity.

In a top-secret operation, code named "vaca loca," Navy SEALs will airlift Denmark's 475,000 cows in 6 Apache helicopters and drop them at the undisclosed location. "We're a little worried about the Holstein. We know that the Red Dane and the Jersey are pretty docile though." The whole operation is expected to last eighteen minutes. "Based on our experience with bin Laden, it should be smooth. We don't expect any enemy fire from the Danes. To tell you the truth, I don't even know if they have an army," said a Pentagon official. To make sure that all goes well, the operation will take place while the Danish televise the killing of the next giraffe. "Everybody will be glued to their TV sets at that time," predicted our source.

As rumors spread about "vaca loca," the Fur Trade Association is already upset that the Navy is using the politically incorrect name SEALs as operatives. "With all this animal love fest going on, the name SEALs will invoke seal slaughter, and before you know it, we will have a bunch of seal lovers protesting all over the place about fur coats."

Given the pernicious global repercussions of Danish barbarism, the UN is considering sanctions against Denmark. The security council is considering a number of actions to bring Denmark in line with the ethical standards of the international community:

- Banning herring for twelve months.
- Disallowing the use of bicycles to go to work.
- Removing the philosophical essays of Søren Kierkegaard from libraries around the world.
- Replacing Tuborg with Miller Lite at restaurants around the Copenhagen zoo.
- Stripping Hans Christian Andersen of his Danish citizenship.
- Turning soccer fields into rehabilitation grounds for wounded giraffes.
- Military invasion.

Efforts are also under way to block incendiary websites such as the animal kill counter. The website claims that in the time it takes you to read this piece approximately 350,000 marine animals, 185,000 chickens, 10,000 ducks, 5,600 pigs, 4,000 rabbits, 3,500 turkeys, 2,800 geese, 2,000 goats, 1,650 cows and calves, 105 dogs, 27 horses, 20 donkeys and mules, and 14 camels would be slaughtered by the meat, egg, and dairy industry. May Marius and all these animals rest in peace.

Chapter Three

Mastering Interactions
to Improve Your Relationships

THE LEARNING SIDE

If you had to name a single factor that contributes the most to your well-being, what would it be? Most people who are asked this question place relationships at the very top of their list. Not only do we depend on others for survival, but it's impossible to imagine a meaningful and fulfilling life without other people in it. Relationships are crucial to our physical survival and psychological well-being.

Married people are generally happier than single people, and those who feel they have a web of supportive relationships are much better off than those who do not. Loving relationships are associated with lower morbidity, a stronger immune system, and better cardiovascular health.[1] People report higher levels of happiness when they interact with others, and that goes for introverts as well as extroverts.[2] People who confront serious illness or other misfortunes often point to their support system as their most valuable resource.

Your relationships with others can contribute the most to your wellbeing or it can be the source of your deepest misery. Your happiest, most meaningful moments probably involve other people, but so do your saddest, most wretched ones. All of us have struggled with a challenging relationship at some point or another—with partners, family members, friends, or coworkers. The closer the relationship, the greater the gain when it goes well (or the pain, when it goes sour). Marriages have a fifty-fifty chance on average, despite initial high hopes and good intentions. Beyond the romantic sphere, negative relationships in families, workplaces, and communities diminish well-being and cause significant damage.

Good relationships are built on multiple positive interactions over time. They require us to cultivate affirming exchanges with others and to work through the inevitable negative ones. This chapter covers two crucial skills for healthy relationships: connection and communication. Flourishing relationships require both, especially at such times when needs and wishes are at cross purposes. We need to invest in our relationships and communicate positively and constructively if we hope that others will do the same.

Connect

Imagine that someone asked you for a word of wisdom on how to become healthier and happier. The challenge is that your wisdom must be distilled in literally one word. What would you say? For me, Ora, that single word of wisdom would be "connect." We spend 80 percent of our waking hours with other people, and our well-being is inextricably tied to the quality of our relationships.

When people believe that the quality or quantity of their relationships do not meet their need for connection, they feel lonely and distressed.[3] Prolonged loneliness is detrimental to physical and psychological well-being. Multiple studies have come to this same conclusion. Lack of social ties is so pernicious that it is more harmful to our health than smoking or obesity.[4] It's not that we simply need relationships with others, but that we need affirming and supportive ones. Relationships marked by high conflict is definitely not what the doctor ordered for our physical or mental health.

If toxic relationships and loneliness are an impediment to wellness, close and supportive ones can be the gift that keeps on giving.[5] I, Ora, live with muscular dystrophy, a progressive and debilitating condition that leads to ongoing physical impairment. I'm nonetheless happy for the most part, which I largely attribute to my social circle, in general, and my marital relationship in particular. Isaac has been my husband, lover, best friend, confidant, coparent, coauthor, and entertainer for nearly thirty-five years. I could not have chosen a better father for our now thirty-year-old son, Matan, whom we love more than life itself. Our relationship is a strong arsenal with the power to dampen the physical and psychological pain of physical decline. The fact that Isaac makes me laugh after all those years is the icing on the cake.

Invest in What Matters Most

We are wired to connect and cooperate. Our very existence depends on it. Nature has equipped kittens, puppies, infants, and other newborns with an irresistible appeal. Their sweetness, softness, and helplessness elicits parental care that is essential to their existence.

Beyond physical survival, responsive and supportive caregiving leads to healthy attachments with lifelong benefits to physical and emotional health.[6] For human babies who take the longest to develop, loving interactions with parents provide the foundation for learning and development. Healthy connections are essential nutrients for the developing brain.

We are social creatures from the moment of birth and continue to thrive on positive interactions and messages that signal belonging and acceptance. Our social nature—our ability to understand others, predict their behavior, and cooperate with them—has given us an evolutionary leg up.[7] It also makes us acutely sensitive to potential exclusion or other social threats.

In fact, social rejection is akin to physical pain, whereas social strokes are like chocolate for our brain.[8] We need to belong,[9] we need others to like us, we need affection and support, and we do best when we lead connected lives. Due to our prosocial human nature, we also get a high from helping others, so it's not all about us—thank goodness for that!

When my son was in prekindergarten at the age of four, I was early to pick him up one day. He was engrossed in play, which gave me an opportunity to observe him interacting with his peers. It only took a few moments for me to notice another four-year-old boy named Nathan. Nathan was stocky and taller than the rest. He stood out though, less because of his size than to his lack of inclusion in the children's play.

To the best of my recollection (it was more than twenty-five years ago), Nathan was not teased or actively excluded; just ignored. The preschool teacher confirmed my hunch that Nathan was struggling to make friends. On the way home in the car, I suggested that we invite Nathan over for a playdate. Matan's initial response from the backseat went something like this: "But if I play with Nathan, other kids won't want to play with me." I remember being startled that a child who still needed a booster seat was so acutely sensitive to the social pecking order. If my memory serves me right, we did find a way of arranging a playdate with Nathan without catastrophic social consequences.

We are wired to connect and thrive on relationships but lead increasingly less social lives.[10] We are less likely than in the past to live close to friends and family, spend time socializing, or report having access to close confidants. There is an abundance of compelling data that should convince us to rethink how we spend our time and effort, especially those who have the good fortune to be financially stable.

Where your health and happiness are concerned, spending more time with important others or volunteering in your community are probably a better investment of your time than working to create more wealth.[11] Even a fraction of the available data should propel you to reflect on your own social bonds.

- The health benefits of having a friend that you see most days is equivalent to the health benefits of having an additional $100,000 a year.[12]
- For nurses diagnosed with invasive breast cancer, a large in-person social network was associated with a four-fold likelihood of survival.[13]
- Among Harvard men followed up over a seventy-five-year period, those who reported being most satisfied with their relationships at age fifty were the healthiest at age eighty.[14]
- Some public health experts believe that given the clear health benefits of volunteering, doctors should recommend it alongside exercise and diet.[15]
- Social engagement and supportive relationships are associated with lower rates of memory problems and dementia among the elderly.[16]

I'm guessing that what you have just read is not entirely new to you. Studies that attest to the health benefits of supportive relationships are frequently reported in the media. Besides, your own lived experience likely aligns with such findings. If you think about situations when you are most happy and fulfilled, they probably involve positive interactions with others.

This is definitely the case for me. Nonetheless, as I write about the value of relationships, I find myself reflecting on how I invest my time and effort. I believe I have high interpersonal well-being and know beyond a shadow of the doubt that close relationships contribute the most to my happiness. I also know that helping other people gives me more satisfaction than almost anything.

All that said, I'm acutely aware that I don't always put my money where my mouth is or where my heart is. I invest in my closest relationships, but I can also get so busy that I neglect to keep in active touch with good friends. I sometimes take on projects or agree to do things that result in less face-to-face time than is ideal for me. This includes making more times for friends, but more important perhaps, being more involved in volunteer efforts in my community. I believe this is the best investment I can make.

Exercise: Check Your Investment Portfolio

What about you? I invite you to check your own social investment portfolio.

- How pleased are you, overall, with the quality and quantity of relationships in your life?
- Are you investing as much as you should in your important relationships? Are you getting enough social time? If not, what gets in the way?
- What would be the impact of changing your investment portfolio? What would you do and how would you do it?

Mind the Positivity Ratio of Relationships

If relationships can be the source of what is best and worse in life, we need to maximize the good and minimize the bad. I realize how ridiculously simplistic this sounds; I can almost hear the collective "duh!" of the reader. No rational person would argue with this logic. At the same time, this simple truism is something that is often neglected as people go about their daily interactions in families, workplaces, and communities. We know in theory that positive relationships are good for us and negative ones are toxic, but we often fail to consider their most crucial building blocks.

The simple fact is that an ongoing relationship between two people is built on the various interactions they have over time. These exchanges vary in valence, duration, and intensity, and many moments of contact are mundane and seemingly inconsequential. But these moments add up and contribute to the overall flavor of the relationship. The ultimate "goodness" or "badness" of a relationship is largely based on the balance of positive to negative interactions.[17] Not only is there compelling research to back this up, but it also makes good sense. It is impossible to go through life without conflict, and trying to avoid it altogether is not only futile but counterproductive. At the same time, it is difficult to envision a good relationship with someone you are in perpetual conflict with—be it your spouse, child, coworker, or neighbor. So if the many moments of interaction are adversarial, the flavor of the relationship is unappealing if not downright foul.

Consider your own experience with some of your best and worst relationships thus far. Bring to mind a person in your own life, in the present or in the past, whom you have felt most positive about. Close your eyes and take a moment to think about this person. What stories, thoughts, and images come to mind? If you feel comfortable, do the same for someone at the opposite end of the spectrum with whom you have had a decidedly negative relationship.

As you consider some of your best and worst relationship partners, you probably recount multiple interactions you have had with them and the related thoughts and feelings. This holds particularly true for those we interact with the most, such as with immediate family members.

It doesn't take a genius to know that if relationship partners spend much of their time together in strife, the relationship will be a negative one overall. It will impede and diminish well-being, rather than facilitate and enhance it. Furthermore, when it comes to marriages and other committed relationships, it's not enough to maintain an equal balance of positive and negative interactions.

According to decades of research by Dr. John Gottman,[18] stable marriages are characterized by a minimum of five positive exchanges for every unpleasant one. Those in close and supportive unions experience so many positive interactions that their positivity ratio is much higher than that.[19] They communicate frequently, know each other well, share of themselves, and take an interest in their partner. They have multiple verbal and nonverbal exchanges throughout the day that keep them emotionally connected. This connection serves as an emotional savings account that enables couples to weather marital conflict and overcome negativity.

Learn from Relationship Masters and Disasters

Of all the relationships that people are embedded in, those between romantic partners have most captivated our attention from time immemorial. It is thus not surprising that it is this relationship (marriage in particular) that has been studied most by relationship scientists. In my teaching experience, few classes are more engaging to students than those that pertain to love and intimacy. Over the years, I have posed the following question in class using an electronic response system: Getting married or having a life-long intimate relationship is part of my life plan.

A. yes
B. no

Almost all students answer this in the affirmative, and the vast majority of them say that they want to marry one day. They say this with a great degree of confidence, even though they are in their late teens or early twenties and are in no hurry to tie the knot anytime soon. Chances are high that they will marry at some point because 90 percent of us do. [20]

For the majority of people, being married is associated with greater life satisfaction, more happiness, and better health. In fact, relative to other demographic factors such as age, race, and even income, being married confers greater benefits to our health and happiness. Multiple studies, including one of our own, [21] have come to the same conclusion.

Marriage is not for everyone and is not the only path to wellbeing or intimacy, but most of us want it and do it, some a few times over. We yearn for that special person who will be our lover, soulmate, confidant, and best friend for the rest of our life. We envision the thrill of being our true selves, known completely, and loved for who we are.

We think about someone who we will completely trust and who will always have our back—literally, and metaphorically—and we want to be that loving, supportive and trust-worthy person for our life partner. As we well know, things don't always turn out that way. And while a good marriage will bolster your well-being, a disastrous one will likely diminish it.

Dr. John Gottman is best known for his ability to predict divorce years in advance with a high degree of accuracy. If this sounds like voodoo to you, you should know that Gottman and his team have a multitude of data to back up their claims. They have done this time and time again, by recruiting couples that agree to spend the weekend in a retreat-like lab.

Couples are told to go through their usual weekend routines; the difference is that they are videotaped and wear monitors that measure their heart rates, blood pressure, and other physio-logical indicators. Couples are asked to have a conversation about a topic that is conflictual in the relationship. Within fifteen minutes of that conversation, researchers detect the telltale signs of healthy and unhealthy relationships, those that are likely to last, and others that are expected to implode. [22]

What do you think are the telltale signs that a relationship is headed for future trouble? What can Gottman and his team pick up from a fifteen-minute marital exchange?

My guess is that your guess is not far off the mark. Couples in troubled relationships fight a lot and fight harshly. In fact, a harsh startup of a conflict conversation is the first sign of trouble, which can be detected from the get-go. In studies that include monitoring bodily responses such as heart rate and blood flow, there are clear indications that the parties in-volved are physiologically flooded—as if they had encountered a tiger in the savanna. That's how our system, which was designed to detect physical danger, responds to situations that are socially threatening, albeit not necessarily dangerous.

The so-called "disaster couples" [23] have other toxic "defend–attack" features to their con-flict interaction: global criticism of the person (rather than specific complaint about a behav-ior), sarcastic comments and/or nonverbal displays of contempt, or defensiveness and/or dis-engagement of one in response to the other's attack. In addition, these couples have a dearth of positivity in their relational bank account. They have not accumulated a large enough reserve of affirming and constructive interactions that can compensate for the low points.

I witnessed the relationship disasters firsthand in my parents' almost forty-year-long mar-riage. By the time they divorced, they had three grown kids who were married and with children of their own. Theirs was a generation that espoused staying together at almost any expense. While divorce is not without consequences and should not be taken lightly, toxic relationships also exact a price.

I have very few memories of positive interactions between my parents and many memories of marital strife and strain. My father would shout while my mother would shut down. Fights would erupt, followed by disengagement, sometimes for days on end. I don't know how old I was, but I distinctly remember my resolve that I would never remain in a miserable relationship.

I'm sure that had my parents worn unobtrusive monitors like the participants in the Gottman studies, there would have been clear indications of physiological flooding. Theirs was a highly conflictual relationship. I know that my mother, who ultimately ended the marriage, would not have done so had there been less strife.

She would have settled for a calm if unhappy marriage, but she could no longer take my father's combativeness. Being of a different generation and character, I knew that this is something I could never settle for. Remaining in a lonely and loveless relationship seemed far worse than living alone, even in the absence of perpetual strife.

Nasty conflict is bad, but its absence is not sufficient for marital bliss. In the Gottman studies, the high conflict couples had a 90 percent chance of divorcing in the first five to seven years of marriage. Some years later, researchers identified another pattern that has important implications to relational well-being. They turned their attention to a subset of couples that raised children together but divorced later in life.

Unlike their early divorcing counterparts, these couples do not necessarily have a highly conflictual relationship marked by escalating fights and attack–defend behaviors. Couples who divorce in midlife are more likely to do so due to an absence of connection than the presence of intense strife.[24] Their relationship suffers from a paucity of friendship, affection, curiosity, and joy. I know I'm not the only people-watcher who notices couples in restaurants that appear to share a table and a meal, but little else. Some of these couples are among my contemporaries and probably yours as well.

Spotting the emotionally connected couples is a lot more fun. Of course, almost everyone seems deeply in love in the early stages of a relationship when brains are awash in endorphins (i.e., happy hormones) and one's romantic partner is seen through rose colored glasses. But what if the couple seated at the table next to you has long passed that initial star struck stage? What clues would indicate a close bond?

It doesn't cease to impress and delight me how quickly this can be spotted in some cases. There are multiple indications that can signal this connection—a smile, a brief touch, an engaged conversation, or a playful expression. It doesn't have to be profound; subtle indications of connection are probably a lot more common, but these little moments add up and form an emotional bank account that grows over time. And just like a savings account can help you weather an unanticipated cost, a relational positivity account can buffer the inevitable moments of relational strain.[25]

When couples do things that nurture their friendship and strengthen their bond, they contribute to their relational account. This entails saying and doing things that makes the other person feel valued and loved. It's about taking a keen interest in your partner, knowing what they value, and understanding their inner psychological world. It's about supporting their goals, focusing on what they are doing right, and expressing affection and appreciation. It's also about being responsive to your partner's attempts to connect with you or to come back from a negative exchange.

John Gottman refers to this as a bid for connection. Bids are attempts to reach out to the other person and connect on an emotional level. It can take different forms, from turning to your partner for support when under stress, to reaching over for a cuddle or touch, to pointing to a pretty bird flying by. Relationships are built bid-by-bid, big and small. The way we respond to bids are crucial because they signal that we either want emotional connection or we don't. The more responsive we are to these bids for connection, the higher the likelihood that we will build a reservoir of positive experiences in the relationship.

Consider a relationship that is dear to you. This can be with a romantic partner or with a very close friend or family member. What do you do to nurture this relationship? How do you and your partner signal your wish to connect? How do you respond to one another's bids? What more can each of you do to strengthen the bond and deepen the friendship? What gets in the way?

Cultivate Flourishing Relationships

The field of relationship science has provided us with important insights that can guide our efforts to build optimal relationships. This is particularly important when it comes to our closest relationship partners. First and foremost, healthy and health-enhancing unions require a safe and supportive foundation. This is best accomplished when partners are perceived through a benevolent and generous lens. If this is your lens, you tend to see behaviors that you like as consistent with your partner's good character and good intentions.

When your partner does something you don't like, you are more likely to see it as temporary and changeable.[26] A tough day at the office, a traffic jam, or a bad mood can have an unfavorable impact on behavior. It doesn't mean that you excuse this conduct or refrain from addressing it, but you do so from this benevolent stance.

A favorable view of one's partner goes hand-in-hand with setting high standards for your own behavior. A value-driven commitment to supportive and constructive interactions will serve you in good stead. When this is consistently (if not perfectly) reflected in your behavior, your partner is more likely to respond in kind. This is the best bang for your buck, as it can help you build the relationship you aspire to have.[27] Undoubtedly, this is easier in some cases than in others and can feel downright impossible in certain situations. It is impossible to be supportive and constructive 100 percent of the time, but this should not prevent you from using it as a moral compass and a framework for behavior. Your partner is likely to respond in kind and to be more forgiving when you fall short.

This may sound obvious, yet simplistic. After all, people have different temperaments and personalities, some more easy-going and agreeable than others. We don't exactly check those in at the relationship door. Furthermore, not everyone had the good fortune of having supportive and responsive parenting early in life, one that fosters a secure attachment to caregivers and a healthy working model for perceiving self and others.

Nonetheless, supportive relationships can undo or attenuate some early damage, and people with more challenging temperaments can learn to better manage their emotions and behaviors. We should not dismiss or downplay the importance of early history or individual differences, but neither should we perceive them as deterministic. Research with romantic partners and college roommates suggests that irrespective of early experiences, prior rejection, or self-esteem, a compassionate stance and a commitment to constructive and supportive behavior can have a favorable impact on relationships.[28]

Consider what this means in the context of your life. What are some specific examples when you enacted this in your interactions? To what extent does it reflect your general approach to relationships? On a scale from 1–10, with 10 being the most supportive and constructive, and 1 being the least, how would you rate yourself? What would you need to do to increase your self-rating by a single point? What difference can this make to your relationship partner? What would it take for someone other than yourself to notice a change for the better? What barriers could get in the way, and how can you address them?

Loving and supportive relationships can serve as a safe haven when people encounter stressful situations and adverse circumstances, but in addition to buffering stress, it can be a secure base from which to navigate the world, deal with setbacks, and take action that can facilitate growth. It's easier to take a risk knowing that our support system is available should we need it. It can embolden us to act when it is constructive for us to do so.

Furthermore, it is much easier to persist with something you want to change in your life when those closest to you are there to cheer you on. Whether it's persevering with a challenging course of study, improved eating habits, or an exercise routine, support and encouragement can make a world of difference.

But relationships that boost health and happiness and facilitate growth need to be nurtured. No less important than support and compassion when your partner is down is the ability to celebrate their successes and partake in their joy when they are up.[29] In fact, some research suggests that how you respond when things go well has important implications for the quality of your relationship.

Sharing good news and proud moments boosts happiness, and having important others share our excitement can increase and extend it. Such gifts need to be reciprocated, and admiration and appreciation should go in both directions. It is worth remembering that just as social rejection can cause pain akin to a physical injury, a social stroke can be a lot more valuable than a tangible reward. When it comes to close relationships, frequent expressions of appreciation, along with abundant displays of affection, can go a long way.

Finally, minding a relationship requires attention to the needs of each individual. Just as we have an innate need for relationships, we yearn for personal autonomy and for experiences of mastery and self-competence. This is the basis for self-determination theory, a well-known psychological theory that has been extensively studied.[30] Supporting our partner's freely chosen and valued goals can promote their growth, increase their self-efficacy, and be supremely rewarding. It will also contribute to your joint relationship bank account and enhance the likelihood that you will be on the receiving end of such support.

In addition, the human need for expansion can also be met by joint novel activities that spark enthusiasm and promote growth. It can also infuse the relationship with a jolt of positive energy and enjoyment. And speaking of enjoyment, nothing is more fun for me than the inside humor we share in our family—the harmless teasing, ridiculous role-plays, and other song and dance. Only our son, Matan, knows how outrageous we can be and how much fun we have as a result.

Consider the Power of Social Support

Yesterday evening, I spoke with my friend Sara over WhatsApp. Sara and I met in a graduate research course at the University of Toronto over twenty-two years ago. It was the first class of the semester, and we happened to sit next to each other. As soon as Sara introduced herself, I detected an unmistakable Israeli accent. Her English was impeccable, but one Israeli can spot another in no time. After a few more words, we discovered that we were both in the doctoral program in counseling psychology and were mothers to young children.

My son was seven years old at the time, and Sara, who is three years my junior, had a two-year-old daughter. Beyond shared heritage and circumstances, we enjoyed each other's company and became friends. We stayed in touch when the course ended and visited each other's homes with our spouses and children. We maintained some contact as our family moved from Canada to Australia and then to the United States. When we moved to Miami, Sara came to visit once with one daughter, then with the other.

A few years ago, Sara was diagnosed with breast cancer. Several weeks after I received her initial email informing me of her diagnosis, she began sending updates in a group email to friends and close associates. Sara is a psychologist in private practice and has been a part of a peer supervision group for many years. Her fellow therapists, most of whom are physicians, have become her friends. Sara included members of that group as well in her email thread. Pretty soon, we would get regular updates on Sara's battle with "Nasty"—that's the name she gave the tumor that invaded her breast and disrupted her life.

As her treatment progressed, Sara genuinely shared her cancer journey; she did not avoid its messier components, nor edit out pain and struggle. She sent pre-chemo pictures from the hairdresser's as she changed hairstyles from long to short, including one in between. She shared the stress she and her husband Roni had endured as they were contemplating different hospitals, surgeons, and treatment plans.

Sara sent feisty emails chronicling her battle with "Nasty," which combined candid descriptions of treatment effects along with humorous anecdotes. She referred to the beginning of treatment as the "unleashing of the firing squad" targeting "Nasty." In time, Sara replaced the battle metaphor with one of transformation. She embraced physical changes with colorful wigs; this way, she said, cancer wouldn't recognize her.

I felt privileged to be among those Sara shared her experience with. Besides, she is an excellent writer and her spirited and humor-laced entries were a pleasure to read. I cherished Sara's updates, and I know others did as well. Friends cheered her on, offered to attend chemo sessions, and they made themselves available in other ways. This could be any of us, and we wanted to envelop her in support.

Indeed, social support is one of the most powerful buffers to stress known to man (and especially to woman), with overwhelming evidence that attests to its ameliorative impact.[31] The few places where men live as long as women are ones where close-knit family and community ties are a way of life.[32] The chances of dying prematurely are so strongly related to social isolation and lack of support that it should be regarded as a health hazard. For women with breast cancer, support by family and friends are associated with a more favorable response to treatment and better outcomes.[33]

Sara's doctorate is in psychology (not medicine), so her physician friends were a great resource when she needed medical information. This type of assistance is known as "informational support." Other friends provided instrumental support—they accompanied her to chemo sessions and provided home-cooked meals. Her best friend, Orna, herself a breast cancer survivor, came from Israel for a few weeks.

The two have been bosom buddies since middle school, and having Orna there was an incredible source of emotional support. Roni, Sara's husband of over twenty-five years, was a pillar of strength throughout. He even learned how to administer the required injections following chemo sessions.

Imparting valuable information, offering tangible assistance, and providing emotional sustenance are three key forms of helping. They are referred to in the literature as informational, instrumental, and emotional support.[34] I like even more their dubbing as "gifts of the head, the hand, and the heart." It's a reminder that there are different ways to be helpful and one person doesn't have to (in fact, cannot) meet all of the support needs.

We all have something to offer and are both the givers and receivers of support throughout life. The gift metaphor is no less important, irrespective of which end you happen to be on.

Social support is a two-way gift, and receivers are not the only beneficiaries. As receivers, knowing that we have people who love and cherish us so much that they will go to great ends to support us, is an affirmation of our own value. This is in addition to the tangible benefits that can ensue, which can make a huge difference.

As givers, we are gaining as well; ample and converging evidence attests to the health enhancing and happiness making qualities of helping.[35] I suspect you don't need research to convince you of this since you have experienced the emotional boost of positively contributing to the life of others.

Think about a time when someone did something that was highly beneficial to you. Who was that person and what did he or she do? What difference did it make in your own life? What does this say about the two of you as individuals? If this is someone who is close to you, what does it say about your relationship?

Now think about a time when you did something that had a large and positive impact on another person. What did you do and how did you do it? How do you know that what you did made a difference? What was that like for you?

In studies that instructed some participants to do three fun things a day, and others to perform three acts of kindness a day, the benefit to the latter was evident.[36] Doing things to support and benefit others is good for our physical, psychological, and spiritual well-being, not to mention our interpersonal and social well-being. I think this is particularly noteworthy given how difficult it can be for many people to accept help, myself included.

Notwithstanding the high I get when I'm able to help someone else, with the exception of a few close others, I struggle when I am on the receiving end of the equation. So much so that one friend asked me if she has to call me every single day to ask if she can give me a ride somewhere now that I am no longer able to drive. When I spoke with Sara the other day and asked for her permission to share her story, she also referenced the challenge of accepting help.

We live in an individualistic society that exalts independence, but this is merely an illusion, and a harmful one at that. We depend on other people as they depend on us, and no one can go it alone. We should thus consider seeking and accepting support as indications of resourcefulness and strength, and not the opposite. Yesterday's receiver is today's giver, and vice versa. Social support is a social good—often reciprocated, frequently paid forward, and advantageous for all.

Communicate

Good relationships bolster health and happiness, while toxic ones and lack of support have a corrosive impact. Constructive communication is key to healthy relationships, as it is the mechanism through which social exchange takes place. We communicate verbally as well as nonverbally, intentionally as well as unintentionally. We communicate with our words, our facial expressions, and our body language. We sometimes say things we later wish we left unsaid; other times, the way something is interpreted is different from what we intended to convey. In short, communication is a complex process and various barriers can get in the way.

On the positive side, it is also a skill that is highly amenable to improvement. Reflecting on how you communicate with others and what you can do to increase its effectiveness can lead to meaningful relational gains. Given everything we know about the importance of good relationships, it is also an important vehicle to flourishing well-being.

Practice Good Listening

Think about a situation when someone did a good job listening to you. What did the person say and do? What made him or her a good listener? Now think about a situation when someone did a poor job listening to you. What did the person say and do? What made him or her a poor listener?

The importance of good listening cannot be overstated. Nonetheless, people worry far more about their *speaking* skills than about their *listening* skills.[37] Even though we spend a good part of our day listening to others, formal training in good listening is the exception rather than the rule. Public speaking is one of the most popular courses on college campuses.

Many students (and professionals!) worry about their presentation skills, but few are concerned about their listening skills. Most of us can easily recount experiences when we were on the receiving end of poor listening. At the same time, we generally regard ourselves as good listeners. So who are these poor listeners? Could they be us?

The truth is that there are many roadblocks to good listening:[38]

- We don't listen well when we are tired, bored, or hungry.
- We don't listen well when we are preoccupied with other issues and fail to focus our attention on the speaker.
- We don't listen well when we have preconceived notions about the speaker based on gender, ethnicity, education, or other attributes.
- We don't listen well when we are busy judging the speaker or are only open to hearing certain things and not others.
- We certainly don't listen well when we are rehearsing our own response instead.
- Most important, we don't listen well when we are the ones doing most of the talking!

No one can honestly claim that their listening, at all times, is barrier free. However, if you are aware of these roadblocks, you are in a much better position to do something about them. If your attention has wandered to other issues, you can escort it back. If you catch yourself judging and planning your own response, you can refocus on the speaker. And if you tend to interrupt or are quick to share your own stories or give advice, you can remind yourself that this is not helpful.

Good listeners demonstrate their intent to listen. They face the speaker, make eye contact, and establish an engaged posture. They listen without interrupting and maintain their attention on the speaker rather than diverting it toward themselves. Even if they think they understand the issue and know how to solve it, they are not quick to jump to the rescue. After all, this may not be what the speaker is looking for. Go back to what you wrote about a time someone did a good job listening to you. Did that person demonstrate any of the behaviors listed above? What about you? Do you enact these behaviors when you are listening?

Keep in mind that we communicate not only with words. In fact, some experts believe that nonverbal communication—facial expressions, tone of voice, and body language—is more important than our words. This is because we are generally more aware and have greater control over what we say than how we say it.

When you listen to someone else, remember to attend to both verbal and nonverbal communication.

- What feelings can you detect from the speaker's gestures and expressions?
- What can you read between the lines?
- Is the speaker's nonverbal communication congruent with his or her words?

You empathize with someone when you can metaphorically place yourself in their shoes, see the world through their eyes, and relate to or even experience their feelings. Of course, we all live in our own skin and can never fully experience the world from another person's vantage point. However, people feel valued when others make an effort to really understand their perspective and relate to their feelings.

In order to empathize, you need to attend not only to what is being said but also how it is said. You need to listen as well as observe. Only then can you attempt to perceive and feel what it is like to be in the other person's shoes.

Being an empathic listener is not simply about accurately perceiving and relating to another's experience. You also need to demonstrate your efforts so that the other person will "feel heard."

For example, these are some of the things you can do:

- Let people talk without interrupting; silence can be golden.
- Nod and show caring with your facial expressions and body language.
- Ask questions to make sure you fully understand the situation.
- Pay attention to facts as well as feelings.
- Check your understanding by summarizing what you have heard and, if appropriate, reflecting feelings that are expressed or demonstrated.
- Suspend judgment and refrain from giving unsolicited advice.
- Stay with the speaker and do not interject with your own stories.

Practice Mindful Awareness and Psychological Flexibility

It's much easier to listen well when you are interested in what the speaker is talking about, but what if you're on the receiving end of a long-winded story suffused with minutiae? Or someone is relaying detailed information you already have? I admit that these are situations that I find particularly challenging; when the impatience I feel inwardly is at risk of manifesting outwardly. This is when I am most at risk of interrupting or trying to move a story along—neither of which I am proud of or try to excuse.

These are not the only occasions when I recognize impatience rearing its ungracious head. It can happen when I wait in line at a store and it seems obvious that lack of efficiency is needlessly holding things up, or when I perceive that one person's inconvenience is caused by another's lack of consideration. It doesn't even have to be me who is inconvenienced! The regular practice of mindfulness has helped me become more aware and accepting of my experience on such occasions. More often than not, it has enabled me to avoid the trap of letting my felt irritation leak out unintentionally.

A mindful awareness and acceptance of moment-to-moment experience can serve as a metaphoric "pause" button. It can create a mental gap between what you think and feel and what you do. The regular practice of mindfulness can enhance self-awareness and create a "window of opportunity" for overriding an unconstructive automatic response.[39] Mindfulness facilitates psychological flexibility—the ability to act from your values even when your thoughts and feelings pull you in a different direction.[40]

This is particularly important in an interpersonal context where goals and needs are sometimes at odds, misperceptions occur, and emotions can become intense. The pretext that someone has "pushed my buttons" is often used to justify negative behavior. In reality, each one of us needs to be in charge of our own buttons and take responsibility when we lose it. When you find it especially difficult to act from your values, it should be a signal that it is particularly important that you do so.

Hear and Be Heard

"He (or she) talks too much"
"He (or she) talks too little"

When you consider people you have regularly interacted with, how many fit each description? My guess is that it is easier for you to make a mental list of those who "talk too much." That is definitely the case for me, even though I recognize that I am at risk of ending up on such a list if I'm not careful!

We connect with others by telling them about important experiences and events in our lives. Opening up to another person is incredibly rewarding and can strengthen the relational bond. Nonetheless, it's important to keep in mind that we are ultimately more interested in our own life than in someone else's life. Thus, a long and detailed story is probably more rewarding to the teller than the listener. Psychological flexibility can help curb the urge to "hog the line" for too long and leave too little space for your communication partner. Boring others with long-winded stories is no way to strengthen a relationship!

A good communicator always has the listener in mind. You may have a wealth of knowledge and information that others can use. If you cannot communicate it effectively, it will be of little use to them. If you are trying to impart knowledge or teach a skill, consider what the listener already knows. Otherwise, you run the risk of overwhelming a novice or boring an expert.

As any parent who has raised a teenager knows, imparting wise advice to the nonreceptive is not very wise. My son taught me this important lesson when he was an adolescent. I learned that holding (at times biting) my tongue made it easier to be heard when it counted the most.

What about you? Can you think of a time when you thought it important to say something but the other person was not open to hearing it? Why do you think that is? In hindsight, how do you assess the situation? What, if anything, might have made the other person more receptive?

Build Bridges and Strengthen Bonds

At times, the most significant messages are those that are most difficult to give and receive. Criticism is something that we simply don't enjoy. This also applies to "so-called constructive criticism, if it's sugarcoated, or if it's dipped in Belgian chocolate and delivered with a dozen roses."[41] Even if you steer clear of the word *criticism* altogether, you may not be able to completely avoid an unpleasant aftertaste. It's better to refer to a concern you want to share, or an issue that you need to address, but it's naïve to assume that a nicer label is all that is needed. At the same time, failure to address problems or discuss sensitive issues has repercussions. For one, it's difficult to come up with optimal solutions without naming and exploring a problem. An unaddressed issue can also fester and "spill out" in a relationship-damaging manner. Just as important, feedback and conflict can be opportunities for individual and relational growth.[42]

It helps to keep in mind that people respond to social threat much the same as to physical threat.[43] Since we are wired to connect and cooperate, messages that signal acceptance and approval are reinforcing, whereas those that convey disapproval are aversive.[44]

I once shared with students my own visceral reaction to a rather innocuous email from a colleague. It was a team email pertaining to a research project we were collaborating on. He wrote, "I disagree with Ora" in response to a suggestion I had made via email. I immediately felt an accelerated heartbeat as I read it. Even though I would've phrased it differently, there was nothing disrespectful nor mean-spirited about my colleague's email. Neither do I ascribe to him any ill intentions, but my visceral reaction is a reminder of the sensitivity some (many?) of us have to critical comments.

This has implications for how to raise sensitive issues and phrase feedback and also how to receive and respond to it. It is particularly significant when it involves people you interact with on an on-going basis. The damage caused by sharp criticism and sweeping comments about the other person's flaws is difficult to undo. Treading gently and framing your concern as specific and solvable increases the likelihood that you will have a receptive partner. Your timing, choice of words, tone of voice, and body language can either put someone on the defensive, or help them feel safe and respected. If you find a good time, calmly describe a specific behavior, explain why it bothers you, and negotiate a joint solution, you're much more likely to resolve the issue and protect or even strengthen the relationship.[45]

When you are providing feedback or raising a sensitive issue, consider the following:

- Check if this is a good time for the other person. If it's not, find a time that will work for both of you and a private space where you will not be interrupted.
- Express your wish to resolve the situation in a manner that promotes the relationship and meets everyone's needs.
- Briefly and calmly describe the behavior that concerned you. Stick with facts and avoid interpretations and generalizations. Stay in the present and refrain from rehashing the past.
- Make "I" comments to describe how you feel and how you are affected by what took place. Explain your understanding of the person's behavior while avoiding accusations and inferences about motives.
- Ask how the other perceives the situation and inquire if there is anything you can do differently. This gives the message that you don't think you are perfect. Be prepared to listen without becoming defensive. Remember to act from values.
- Say what would work better for you and check if this would work for your communication partner. Encourage other ideas and possible solutions.
- Express appreciation for the other's willingness to listen and work jointly on a good outcome.

Many of us say that we want others to tell us if we do something that is hurtful or bothersome. We understand that others may see things that we are currently unaware of and would benefit from knowing. At the same time, it's hard not to feel defensive when one is on the receiving end of critical feedback.

Psychological flexibility allows you to be mindful of your internal experience, yet respond constructively from a valued position. The fact that you feel defensive and have the urge to push back doesn't mean that you need to act on it. In fact, feeling compelled to speak is probably a good indication to keep quiet and listen. Learning how someone was impacted by something you said or did can be highly beneficial.

Often times, conflict results from misunderstandings and misinterpretations. It is highly plausible that your behavior was interpreted very differently from what you intended to convey. Knowing this presents you with an opportunity to explain and clarify. If you discover that your behavior was hurtful or damaging to another person, you have an opportunity to own up, apologize, and do better.

When you are on the receiving end of critical feedback:

- Let the other person speak without interrupting. Listen rather than plan your response.

- Adopt a curious attitude. Ask for details in order to learn and enhance your understanding rather than as a means of challenging the speaker.
- Agree with facts that are accurate.
- Acknowledge that the other person may see things differently than you and is not obligated to see it your way.
- If you realize that you were wrong, apologize and work to change it.

If you sincerely believe in treating people with dignity and respect, you should strive to abide by it irrespective of what others do. Communicating with integrity and making genuine efforts to resolve differences in a relationship-enhancing manner does not guarantee that others will respond in kind. It's important to remember that we can't control other people's behavior but we can focus our efforts on controlling our own. A resolve to be unconditionally constructive can guide your actions in various contexts and interactions.

Recognize, Appreciate, and Celebrate

A wife complains to her husband that it has been ages since he last told her that he loves her. Looking puzzled, he responds: "I told you that I love you when I married you 20 years ago. If anything changes, I'll let you know." This joke makes an important point and applies not only to marriages or close relationships. There is a universal longing to "feel the love"—most crucially by intimates and close family and friends, but also by fellow students, work colleagues, and superiors. Lack of recognition by a superior is one of the key reasons for employee disengagement.

Across the United States, two thirds of the workforce report feeling disengaged, resulting in many negative outcomes for themselves and the workplace. Disengaged workers experience higher stress and lower physical and mental health. In addition to the human cost to workers and families, workplaces pay the price of higher absenteeism, greater turnover, and lower productivity.[46]

Individuals are most likely to thrive and do their best when they feel liked, appreciated, and valued. Feeling valued is a central component of mattering. But for others to feel valued, they have to also feel that they add value, which is the second pillar of mattering. Receiving public, specific, and detailed recognition nourishes the soul. Feeding our need for recognition stimulates our desire to keep adding value to ourselves and others. It is a virtuous cycle.[47]

There are multiple ways to add value to others. Expressing gratitude for a job well done, or for help with a project, can go a long way in nurturing a sense of mattering. The appreciation and recognition we show others is nothing less than spiritual nutrition. Recognition is a wonderful psychological nutrient, and the more specific, expressive, and detailed it is, the more potent this tonic becomes.

It is not enough to praise someone with a "job well done, Tom." We have to articulate what is it that Tom did, how he did it, and what impact it made. It is more like *Thank you Tom for taking the lead on the proposal for the Acme account. You designed the project, wrote most parts of it, consulted with others, incorporated their feedback, and revised the document. I believe the proposal is very strong because of what you did. I feel confident that thanks to your efforts we have a very good chance of getting the business. You worked on this for several weeks and I know you even spent a couple of weekends going over the background materials. You were diligent and conscientious. I'm very thankful for what you did.*

Positive communication not only builds up the recipient, it also strengthens the relationship. The more we deposit positive emotions into our join relationship bank account, the more resilient the relationship becomes, and the easier it is to endure moments of tension and conflict. If we build trust through recognition and appreciation, both parties will feel more secure when honest and even critical feedback is required. Unfortunately, many relationships are built exclusively on critical feedback. This type of connection breeds fear and alienation. Gratitude builds bridges whereas unfettered criticism erodes trust.

Relationships built on mutual appreciation can endure conflict and difficult moments because there is a secure base. There is a reservoir of positive communications that reverberates inside our heads and hearts. The positive memories tell us that "Emily has been very appreciative of my work in the past. If she has some critical feedback, I know it's coming from a good place." To reach this stage of non-defensive communication, we must toil to build a positive ratio of positive to negative interactions. Our ability to sustain criticism is proportionate to the positive communicative deposits into our relational bank account.

To grow the positive communication bank account, we must also grow our lexicon of gratitude and recognition. We must refine our ability to show gratitude. Some methods include:

• Noticing other people's strengths and commenting on them
• Amplifying recognition by doing it publicly
• Asking open ended questions about accomplishments
• Inquiring about how people did what they did
• Catching people being good
• Writing thank-you notes
• Offering people an opportunity to talk about their work and achievements
• Asking people to mentor others
• Giving people an opportunity to document what they did well

It is a mistake to think that only children need praise and recognition. All of us need to feel valued. It is hard to add value when we are not feeling valued. In some respects, recognition is a miracle cure: it is free, it does wonders for recipient and provider alike, and it is renewable.

Lest people think that we might coddle adults by showing them excessive love, we hasten to point out that we should also expect great things from people. Praise and recognition must be earned. Otherwise, they feel inauthentic and feed a sense of entitlement. We must help people make contributions that would earn them recognition. Just like we help our children succeed, we must help our peers, friends, and spouses experience mastery, control, and self-efficacy. Affording them opportunities to refine their mastery over certain tasks is a wonderful gift. But once they master the task, we should not forget to recognize them for it.

We reach out to close others when we are in need of support, but we also want to share our good news and happy moments. Undoubtedly, you've experienced this yourself upon receiving good news that made you want to jump for joy. Perhaps it was that long-awaited acceptance letter to your first choice graduate school. Or it was that promotion you were hoping for; or news that you are pregnant; or that your beloved has agreed to marry you.

There is probably nothing you wanted more at such times than to share your good news with someone close. How did that person respond? Did he or she match your excitement and want to hear all the details? And how did you react when someone shared their happy news with you?

How we respond to others' high moments are in some respects even more important than our reaction in their moments of need. Imagine telling a friend that you have accepted a position in another city that presents you with exciting opportunities. Shelly Gable has identified four different ways of responding to such news.[48] If your friend says "We probably won't keep in touch once you move—it's too difficult to sustain a friendship from afar, this is an example of an active and destructive response. It probably means that losing touch won't be such a loss. How about if your friend simply ignores what you said and diverts attention to another issue? You share your news and get "I have to shop for new clothes for my sister's wedding." This type of a response is passive and destructive. Slightly better (but still deflating) is a response that is passive and constructive. Your big exciting news is met with a "that's nice, congratulations" response that fails to match your enthusiasm or celebrate your accomplishment.

The best response is one that is both active and constructive. "OMG! How exciting! Go back and tell me from the beginning. How did you find out? I want to hear the details about what this new job entails. It doesn't surprise me in the least that you were their chosen candidate. I'll miss having you so close, but I'm so happy for you!" Your friend's enthusiasm matches or even exceeds your own. His tone of voice, facial expressions, and body language are all consistent with his complementary and celebratory words. This type of communication nourishes the spirit and strengthens bonds.

THE LAUGHING SIDE

We need to learn two interaction skills that are essential for well-being: connect and communicate. Achieving high levels of dexterity in self-expression and empathy is not as easy as it sounds. Conveying your feelings and thoughts with accuracy in succinct form is a rare art. I know so many people who get totally lost in details before they get to the point. And guess what? The more they associate with each other, the longer they all take to get to the F&!@$ point!

I know a few people who can take 45 minutes to tell you something that most human beings can communicate via twitter. As I listen to them politely and begin to feel the equivalent of a piranha attack in my whole body I can't help but think:

* I wonder if I can pretend that I'm having a heart attack
* Where is the nearest sanatorium?
* Can somebody please lobotomize this person?
* Pass me the cyanide
* And you wonder why you're lonely?

I know that I should appreciate diversity and empathize with these long-winded people and all that, but for the love of God, can somebody please tell them to get to the frigging point? Don't they know that the fastest route to a destination is a straight line? Fortunately, most people are not so long-winded and can get to the point relatively quickly. For these deserving people, like your children, you need to practice empathy.

Empathy and Chutzpah

When I was building my family, I was all for promoting self-expression. I was all for women's liberation and children's liberation. I wanted my wife and son to feel free to express their views and feelings. BIG MISTAKE!

As a result of my foolishness, I have spent the last thirty years surrounded by overly assertive family members who challenge my every word, question my judgment, and want me to experiment with colors other than brown. Our son never had a thought that didn't find its way into his mouth. My wife, in turn, never had a gripe she didn't express. Oh, the joys of democracy.

But I have to admit that both have made me a better person: more empathic, more sensitive, more egalitarian, more democratic, more in tune with my feelings. So much so, that I can never speak to male friends anymore. So much so, that every major decision in the house, like the color of my underwear, requires a meeting with minutes and secret ballot.

Coping with assertive family members has been excellent training for dealing with students and faculty members. The other day, and this is a true story, I received an email from a student at another university telling me that his psych professor had assigned them a paper that I had written. The assignment entailed reading the article and writing a critique. The student had the chutzpah of asking me to write a few points critiquing my own bloody paper! I hadn't heard such chutzpah since the son who killed his parents asked the judge for leniency because he was an orphan.

Mastering interactions is basically about two things: expressing your ideas respectfully, and listening attentively. During my career I have been in too many meetings where neither was present. In one corner, you have the rantologist who, no matter what the topic is, will always rant about his pet peeve. In faculty meetings, this is usually the worst teacher, who has not published anything since getting tenure 35 years ago, complaining about lack of standards. In the other corner, you have the repeatologist, who must repeat everything four times to feel satisfied. And then there is me, going crazy.

When I was building my team at work, I was all for promoting self-expression. I was all for employee participation, student voice, faculty engagement. I wanted faculty, students, and staff, to express their views. HUGE MISTAKE! What got into my head?

No places in universities are better than faculty meetings to display the prowess of rantologists and repeatologists. I happened to be Dean of Education and Human Development, and because all professors went to school supposedly, they all feel like they could run the school, which is pretty much like saying that because I went to the doctor I could run the Medical School, or because I live in a house I could run the School of Architecture, but that logic escapes faculty members. Such display of machismo makes the NRA envious, and all in the name of enlightenment and erudition of course.

There is family, there are colleagues, there are students, and then, of course, there are Miami drivers. Mastering interactions with each is no small feat. Going to faculty meetings is good training for driving in Miami. Whereas my wife and my son have made me more sensitive, empathic, democratic, egalitarian, and in tune with my feelings; faculty meetings have made me more dictatorial, despicable, insensitive, and authoritarian; which is great for dealing with Miami drivers.

The Evolution of Thank You

As we were leaving, I held the door open for the couple coming into the restaurant. Neither said thank you though, which wouldn't have surprised me had they been from Miami, but they looked from the North East. Don't ask me how, but I just knew it. I could tell they were pretentious because of their clothing, perfume, watches, shoes, glasses, hairdo, height, accent, and eyelashes. They had an arrogant flair that comes only from certain parts of New England. Their rudeness was distinct from Miami rude, which is less haughty and more egotistical.

Whereas Northerners actively ignore you, Miamians actively attend only to themselves. Whereas the former signal "you're beneath me," the latter signal "you're beneath my augmented breasts. I can't see you. Get out of there!"

According to evolutionary theory, people are nice to you only if they think they will ever need you, which explains why a lot of people in Miami are only nice to plastic surgeons and judges. If you fall in neither category you can forget about civility, which is why I'm considering going to law and medical school, which would be easier than instilling manners in Miami-Dade County.

I would have thought that going into Thanksgiving, folks would be a little more courteous, a little more generous, but everybody is going crazy. People are more dangerous than ever, especially, but not only, to turkeys. Take George Zimmerman, the poor soul is experiencing attacks from everyone: the media, prosecutors, former girlfriends; even the NRA is after him for giving the organization a bad name.

Nobody says thank you George for leaving no more weapons in the stores. No wonder he is reacting aggressively. Or take Richard Incognito from the Miami Dolphins. Nobody thanked him for self-disclosing a very bad case of arrested moral development. Instead of thanking George and Richard for giving newspapers what to write about, all they get is bad press.

Not to be outdone, the Republicans refused to say thank you to President Obama for handing them the easiest exit strategy from their government shutdown debacle a few years ago. Instead of thanking him for the botched launch of HealthCare.gov, they accused him for failing to start something they desperately wanted to stop.

Intrigued by the whole thank you thing I did some research into civility. In a highly publicized study, true story, Dacher Keltner and his research team at UC Berkeley reported that rich people are less polite and more inconsiderate than people from low socioeconomic status. While you might be tempted to believe the findings because they come from BERKELEY, to me the whole thing sounds like a communist plot. This is yet another attempt to disparage the wealthy. After all, this study was done at BERKELEY, which, need I remind you, is a hotbed of radicalism. To be convinced, I would want to have the study replicated by the Heritage Foundation.

To probe further, I did some research into the history of thank you. The first person to ever say thank you was Adam. He had to go to the toilet and asked Eve for the only leaves that up to that point were covering her private parts. He said "thank you" and she said "I hope the paparazzi are not around."

The Jewish people had a conflictive relationship with "thank you." They were all very appreciative when Moses took them out of Egypt, but complained profusely when they realized that he had taken them on a forty-year journey through the desert on a diet of water and unleavened bread.

The Romans, in turn, forced all their victims not only to surrender, but also to send Thank You cards to the Emperor for enslaving them. This Italian tradition continues to this day. The mafia requests Hallmark Love You cards from businesses under their protection plan.

I also looked into famous thank you lines to see what I can learn from wiser people and found the following from Benjamin Disraeli: *I feel a very unusual sensation—if it is not indigestion, I think it must be gratitude.* Can you imagine being led by such a grouch? No wonder the British Empire has been in decline ever since the twice prime minister was in office in the 1800s.

The most important piece of research I found though was that practicing gratitude is good for you. So here it goes: I'm thankful for living in Miami, I'm thankful for having health insurance through my employer—which I can keep—and I'm thankful for the Nobel Prize committee for considering me, next year.

InTRUMPetation of Historical Events

Some individuals can exert great influence on others. Sometimes they start historical trends. In this story we recount how a teacher remembered the elections of 2016.

The year is 2078. The school is Lincoln High in Mount Dora, Florida. The class is AP American History. The teacher, Ms. Wright, is reviewing early century electoral politics.

To understand what happened during the 2016 presidential election, historians coined the term InTRUMPetation. It was the only way they could make sense of events that year. InTRUMPetation refers to the interpretation of social and cultural developments in light of The Ridiculously Unfit Megalomaniac Politician (not to be confused with The Reprehensible Unhinged Malicious Politician, which was a media conspiracy led by MSBNC, which was eventually bought by the Koch brothers and transformed into the Gas Channel).

Scholars of that era found that politicians fitting the acronym exerted tremendous influence on people. Some of the behaviors observed in the masses involved thought disorders, paranoia, and uncontrolled repetition of words like "disaster" and "lock her up." In addition, many people engaged in excruciating mental pirouettes to convince themselves that it was okay to vote for a ridiculously unfit megalomaniac. These people developed a new disorder that involved the inability to look at themselves in the mirror, creating a whole new industry for glass recycling, which is the only thing the candidate ever did for small businesses.

Personalities reflecting the TRUMP profile set unprecedented trends in society. Some of them include the following:

1. *Change we can fake*: A particular politician spewed venom toward immigrants, demeaned women, stereotyped African Americans and mocked people with disabilities, only to pretend to have become a caring humanitarian when the polls showed that he was becoming as popular as the Zika virus. From that point forward, integrity meant the ability to fake it until you make it. With the advent of TRUMPism, candidates felt they could say one malicious thing one day and fake a change of heart the next; hoping to come across as compassionate, while insisting that they never really changed their position. You figure that out!

2. *Summersault insults*: Candidates afflicted with TRUMPism used every opportunity to hurl summersault insults at minorities. These were offensive comments that, despite the appearance of conciliation, and blatant pandering, reinforced stereotypes, supplanting one insult with another. Nobody before had succeeded in adding insult to injury with such panache.

3. *Plastic smiles:* Supporters of said candidates went through rigorous training to fake plastic smiles during CNN interviews. Large funds were invested in whitening and straightening the teeth of their supporters. If you ever hoped to get a job with these candidates, you had to subject yourself to hours of corrective smiling and painful dentistry.

4. *Surrogate parents*: Political surrogates had to make up excuses for their candidate's behavior, the way parents excuse their son's bullying behavior as "boys will be boys." A new cadre of surrogates emerged whose only job was to rationalize the stupefying behavior of their benefactor. This bogus adulation by surrogates was known to have caused severe vomiting.

5. *Collective Disinhibition Disorder:* Along with surrogates, voters also began making up excuses for what had been, up until that point, inexcusable demeanor such as mocking people with disabilities. In prior elections, the public would have been completely outraged, but TRUMPism changed everything. Scorn was tolerated, misogynist com-

ments were accepted, and vulgarity was celebrated. The candidate legitimized the expression of voters' primitive instincts, suppressing the normal functioning of their prefrontal cortex. This phenomenon had been seen only in Miami before, where 90 percent of drivers don't have a prefrontal cortex whatsoever.

6. *Recurring incoherence*: When questioned about contradictory statements, the subject engaged in repetitive incoherent utterances that, had they been emitted by anybody else, would have landed the person in a psychiatric unit. The level of unintelligibility of his pronouncements was only rivaled by self-referential grandiosity. Supporters, by the way, thought this kind of behavior was awesome. The masses identified with their leader and grew proud of their own vitriol.

7. *Journalistic addictive behavior*: The candidate affected by TRUMPism knew how to draw attention. Every day he would level new preposterous accusations, like the former president of the United States founded ISIS, and the media would rush toward him to verify what he said. This promoted an addictive behavior on the part of journalists that provided free advertising to the candidate, but left reporters feeling more confused than ever before. This pattern of outlandish pronouncements and journalistic obsession became a new form of co-dependence. Day after day, this pattern was repeated until election night.

This concluded Ms. Wright's review of *early century electoral politics*. At the end of her lecture, Angela had a question.

Angela: Ms. Wright, what happened to the TRUMP candidate after the election?

Ms. Wright: After he won the elections, he moved to Russia.

Robbie: Ms. Wright, why did he move to Russia?

Ms. Wright: He loved their president.

Angela: What did he do in Russia?

Ms. Wright: He bought an island in Siberia, built a huge wall to protect himself against immigrants, and asked polar bears to pay for it.

Chapter Four

Mastering Cues to
Improve Your Surroundings

THE LEARNING SIDE

We like to think that everything we do is based on rational decisions, motivation, and will-power, without much regard for external influences. Nothing could be further from the truth.[1] Paying more attention to the cues around us will make us smarter and healthier.[2] In this chapter we will learn to appreciate the power of signals in our environment. Our goal should be to read cues and change cues for personal growth, organizational improvement, and community change.

Read the Cues

If there is a big chocolate bar on your kitchen table, the chocolate bar is talking to you: it's telling you, "Come eat me." If there is a big sale sign at your favorite clothing store, the sign is telling you, "Come in, we'll make you pretty." Our environment is full of cues like these.

Your job is to master the art of reading cues. The better you get at it, the easier it is to improve your life. The problem is that most people are not aware of how cues affect their behavior. They think they can resist drinking too much when they go out with their buddies, but once they're at the bar, surrounded by tons of bottles and people drinking alcohol, their willpower usually diminishes.

Cues, however, are not always negative. There are healthy cues as well, like leaving your jogging clothes next to your bed to remind you to exercise first thing in the morning, or making plans to go for a walk right after work with a colleague. To help ourselves, we have to surround ourselves with healthy cues and we have to eliminate unhealthy ones.

If you open your kitchen pantry and see a bag of your favorite potato chips, your will to resist junk food can be easily overpowered. Show your willpower by *not* bringing home junk food at all. Show your strength by avoiding negative cues altogether.

The environment is always talking to us. Our job is to appreciate what it's telling us. When our environment contains cues that lead us to unhealthy behaviors, we can take charge by making changes to our environment.[3]

Alcoholics Anonymous (AA) and other twelve-step programs teach those who struggle with addictions to pay attention to *people*, *places*, and *things* in their environment. This is because certain locations like bars, certain things like alcoholic beverages, and certain people like their former drinking buddies are triggers for addiction. In some cases, recognizing and limiting exposure to certain people, places, and things can help us resist problems. In other cases, we may not want to avoid certain people but may want to change how their presence cues us to behave in certain ways.

To become a good detective, you have to know that cues come in different types. There are two primary kinds of cues: *subtle* and *blatant*. While the former operate largely at a subconscious level, the latter are pretty obvious and easy to detect. Still, both are difficult to read sometimes. What both types of cues have in common is that they influence our behavior in significant ways.

Blatant Cues

You know that to prevent sexually transmitted diseases you need to wear a condom. You heard this before, from your parents, your doctor, your nurse, your teacher, and your sister. But in the heat of the moment, you forget to do it. When you are hot, you are less likely to behave rationally. The rational option would have been to wear a condom, but in the heat of the moment, passion takes over and rationality goes out the window. This is what Dan Ariely calls a *hot condition*, but just to be clear, hot doesn't apply only to sex,[4] it can also apply to shopping and drinking and many other behaviors.

When you are in a *cold condition*, that is, without a naked person or a bottle of tequila in front of you, it is easier to think about the rational thing to do, such as wearing a condom or drinking only one glass. You know that you should not have unprotected sex with people you just met, and you know that getting drunk can lead to accidents. In a cold state, it all makes perfect sense, but when you are in the heat of the moment, a lot of people tend to behave impulsively.

Ariely asked a bunch of male college students to predict how they would react to a variety of sexual encounters; so far, nothing unusual about this study. But wait. He asked them to make predictions while they were masturbating (yes, he did get approval from the university ethics review committee). While masturbating, obviously a hot condition, they predicted that they would engage in all kinds of irrational behaviors.

When they were asked the same questions in a cold condition, like having a coffee, they said that they would never do such things as having unprotected sex. Temptations and other hot conditions have a way of interfering with decisions that sound rational in a cold state.

If you are ravenous and you just entered a Chinese buffet, chances are that your diet will go out the window. Being famished is a hot condition. No matter how many times you told yourself to exercise restraint in all-you-can-eat buffets, your impulse wins. If you are starving, delay of gratification will stay in the parking lot, along with self-control.

Eating and having sex are pretty blatant cues. You cannot miss the egg rolls and the sexual cues in front of you. There is nothing unconscious about this, but still, in the heat of the moment, it is hard to do the right thing.

Judging by the growing waistline of the average American, many people have problems controlling their eating habits. There is nothing subtle about ingesting a huge bucket of fried chicken and imbibing a gigantic cup of soda. You can touch, feel, and smell the food. You may know cognitively that too much greasy food and too many sugary drinks are not really healthy for you, but the aroma and the habit overpower your self-control every time.

Willpower is no match for the taste of fried chicken, bacon, and fries. This is why Brian Wansink recommends minimizing encounters with these cues to begin with. But if you cannot help it, and you do encounter them, he has plenty of ideas to minimize the negative impact.[5]

Wansink studied the design of healthy and unhealthy kitchens, restaurants, and offices. He wants to help you lose weight by redesigning your environment as opposed to redesigning your brain. Armed with knowledge about what slim people do and what their kitchens look like, he conducted multiple experiments to see if environmental arrangements make a difference. He wanted to see if things such as the size of your plate and the stuff on your counter make a difference in *what* people eat and *how much* they eat.

Well, you guessed it: they make a huge difference. Wansink calls his approach "slim by design," and we highly recommend it. The size of the plate, the location of the TV, the containers for leftovers, and the stuff on the kitchen counter constitute clear cues to eat more or less, to watch TV and keep eating, or to go for the veggie leftovers as opposed to the roast beef. In the next section we summarize Wansink's recommendations to change the cues. If you know what cues will invade your senses—especially in a hot condition, such as when you come home hungry from work—you can control your impulses.

Shopping is another example of a hot condition. You may have said to yourself in a cold condition that you only need to buy a pair of pants, but then you enter Macy's and you see all kinds of things that would look so great on you. You just can't resist buying that dress shirt on sale, to say nothing of the tie that goes along with it. The difference between hot and cold decision making can be thousands of dollars.

Drinking too much, eating too much, having unprotected sex, and shopping too much may be considered situations with *blatant cues*. You see the bottle, the food, and the clothes. These are highly detectable people, places, and things. But in the case of *subtle cues*, it is harder to detect what is influencing your decisions.

Subtle Cues

Consider the famous Asch study in which participants were asked to gauge the length of lines shown on two cards. In the first card participants were shown a line. In the second card they were shown three lines, one of which was exactly the same length as the line on the first card.[6]

The task was pretty simple: which line on the second card is the same length as the line on the first card. Most participants could easily see which of the three lines on the second card was identical to the one on the first. This exercise was done in a group setting, and people could hear what other participants said. In other words, you could hear how other folks were answering the simple task of identifying the correct line on the second card.

As it turns out, seven of the eight people in each group were part of the research team (confederates). Starting on the third round, the confederates were instructed to give wrong answers to see if the true participant in the study would change his mind. A surprising number of true participants, who were asked for their answers after the seven phony participants gave theirs, changed their minds and offered wrong answers; just to be in line with the rest of the group.

In subsequent interviews, the true participants said that although they were confident that they knew which line was the correct one, the collective voice of the group exerted a big influence on their decision.

When other folks make judgments that are different from yours, regardless of how patently wrong they may be, your convictions suffer. People are influenced by the perceptions of others, even when their common sense tells them that they are right and the other people are wrong. We are all highly susceptible to other people's opinions. Conforming to the majority view is a subtle influencer. This is a well-known phenomenon.

Conformity can be innocuous but it can also be hazardous. If there is danger in a room, such as smoke, but nobody does anything and you tend to conform, you are putting yourself and others at risk. This can lead to the *bystander effect*. An emergency may be taking place, but if nobody reacts with alarm, you are less likely to take action yourself. This happens more often than you think. It happened in the famous case of Kitty Genovese in Queens, when neighbors ignored her plea for help as she was stabbed to death by a stranger.[7]

There is nothing subtle about screaming for help, but if nobody else does anything, you tend to think that it may not be such a big deal or that others will take action. When the latter takes place, we talk about *diffusion of responsibility*. You just think others will do something. In cases of conformity, as in cases of bystander passivity, the cues may be subtle (*if others think it's not a big deal, why should I?*), but the consequences grave.

Another type of subtle cue is called *stereotype threat*. Social psychologist Claude Steele discovered that alluding to a stereotype harms the performance and overall well-being of the people in the stereotyped group. For example, if the stereotype that blacks do not do as well as whites in academics is merely insinuated, blacks perform worse than in situations when the stereotype is not brought up.

Similarly, when the stereotype that girls generally do not perform very well in math is summoned, female students end up performing worse than they would if the stereotype hadn't been elicited. Reminding whites that they are not as good as blacks in athletics confirms the stereotype as well. In short, stereotype threat is about the risk of confirming a negative stereotype about one's group when a negative stigma is invoked.[8]

If you belong to a stereotyped group, you should care about this subtle cue because it can affect your occupational, academic, emotional, and overall well-being. But even if you don't belong to a stereotyped group, you should care because it can harm other people. This is a process that takes place mostly at a subconscious level, which is why we call it a subtle cue, but as in the cases of conformity and bystander passivity, it can have serious deleterious effects.

It may be hard to believe that subtle cues such as a comment about race would affect how individuals perform on a test, but it does happen. People's ability is affected by anxiety. We are extremely sensitive to other people's judgments. We get our cues from other people, no matter how irrational these cues might be. Whether we are talking about reporting the length of lines on a card or intervening in an emergency, we first see what other people are doing and then decide what to do ourselves.

We don't like to stand out, and we fear ridicule. This is why we surrender to group pressure, even when our common sense objects to the group's consensus. It may be enough for two or three other people to contradict your views—even when they are wrong—for you to change your mind.

Before other people voiced their opinions in the Asch experiment, participants were absolutely certain which line on the second card corresponded to the one on the first, but as soon as other people contradicted their common sense they fell in line with the majority. This is how individuality is suppressed and how group pressure prevails. This is why some people are afraid to speak up. They are afraid to stand out.

Peer pressure is an important subtle cue, but there are other, barely perceptible things that influence our behavior and judgment. For example, if you are holding a hot cup of coffee, you are more likely to judge a person as warm than if you are holding a cup of ice tea. Similarly, you are more likely to judge a person as a democrat if you are holding a soft ball in your hand than if you are holding a hard object.

You are also more likely to perceive someone as more sexy if they are wearing red. It sounds preposterous, but Thalma Lobel, my former professor, documented in *Sensation: The*

New Science of Physical Intelligence, how different perceptions of smell, temperature, height, touch, color, and weight affect our perceptions of other people and the world. [9]

Presumably, somebody's height should not influence our perception of his competence, but it does. Presumably, touching a rough surface before interacting with a person should not affect our impression of her, but it does. People, places, and things are always exerting an impact on us. If we want to change certain things about our lives, such as how we make decisions, we have to know how these cues operate. If we want to behave more rationally when we go shopping, it would be good to know how marketers are trying to get us to buy things we don't need and pay prices we can't afford.

Social psychologist Robert Cialdini wrote one of the most influential and persuasive books on influence and persuasion. [10] In it he describes several strategies that shrewd marketers use to manipulate our behavior. The first one is the *compare and contrast principle.* If you go to a store to buy a suit and a sweater, the salesperson will show you the suit first. This will help in selling you an expensive sweater. After you pay $650 for a suit, paying $85 for a sweater will not look like much. But if you buy a sweater for $85 first and then you are shown a suit for $650, you are likely to think the second item is too expensive. Real estate agents often show you an overpriced house before they show you the one they want you to buy. By contrasting with the previous one, the one they want you to buy looks much better than if they had shown it to you first.

The contrast principle works wonders sometimes, especially when you are a college student. Cialdini presents a version of the following story. A female college student sends an email to her parents:

> Dear Mom and Dad,
>
> I'm sorry I did not write for a few weeks. Before you keep on reading, I want you to sit down. Please sit down. The last few weeks have been rough. I neglected to tell you that I met a boy when I was at a bar a few weeks ago. He had just been released from jail for drug trafficking, but he is really sweet. He shared with me that he had a venereal disease. He was very honest. It was love at first sight. In the heat of the moment, we had unprotected sex, and I got an infection. I also realized later that I got pregnant from this encounter. In addition, I forgot to pay my health insurance bill and when I went into the hospital for some emergency procedure they charged me $23,750. I asked them to send you the bill.
>
> Now that you've read all these horrible things let me tell you the truth. I did not meet a boy, did not get pregnant, did not have an infection, did not have unprotected sex, and did not go to the hospital, but I did get a "C" in organic chemistry. I hope you can see my poor grade in proper perspective now.
>
> Yours, Emma.

The second principle Cialdini talks about is *reciprocation.* Feeling indebted to a person creates a sense of obligation. As a result, we are more likely to say "yes" to a person who has given us something or has done something for us. This is the secret of "free samples" in stores. Once you accept a free gift you feel the need to reciprocate and are more likely to buy the product associated with the sample. As the saying goes, "There is no free lunch." In the past, members of the Hare Krishna group used to be quite assertive about asking for donations. With time, they understood that people would be more likely to contribute if they give them a rose first.

If we want to resist this subtle form of manipulation it helps to be aware of it, but sometimes the temptation is just too much. Lobbyists and pharmaceutical representatives know only too well the benefits of reciprocity. When lobbyists invite politicians to cocktails at exclusive venues, or pharma reps send doctors to conferences in exotic locations, a sense of obligation builds. Just as there is no free lunch, there is no free trip. Beware of free samples, free lunches, and free trips.

Commitment and *consistency* is another form of subtle manipulation. An experiment in California showed how easy it is to get people to consent to things they would normally object to. Researchers asked neighbors if they would agree to place a small sign on their lawns asking residents to "drive safely." A couple of months later, city officials asked the same neighbors who agreed to place the small sign if they would consent to placing a huge sign with the same safety message.

Despite the fact that the sign obstructed their views and was a huge inconvenience, those who had agreed to place the small sign before were much more likely to place the big sign later. An early commitment to do something creates a need for consistency. "If I already agreed to help the community with a small thing, I should agree with a bigger thing."

Human beings crave consistency. As Cialdini noted, we fool ourselves just to keep our thoughts consistent with previous actions or statements. We detest cognitive dissonance, which is the internal tension created by inconsistency. "If I said *yes* before, and now I say *no* to something similar, it shows that I'm inconsistent." The feeling of inconsistency creates cognitive dissonance. If they object to placing the big sign on the lawn they would feel dissonance between a previous action and a new one.

To eliminate the tension created by the inconsistency, people tended to agree to a big sign, even if it was a colossal inconvenience. What the agreeable residents of California could have done is to say to themselves, "This is different. I could support your cause when it was not inconvenient, but the big sign is going to create a problem for me now. I still support safe driving, but I prefer to do it in ways that do not interfere with the quality of my life."

A strategy to get people to do something is to get them to commit to something small. Once you donate a few dollars to a particular cause it is easier to get you to donate a second time because you want to be consistent with your previous behavior. The mere act of signing a pledge or making a commitment is predictive of future behavior concordant with the promise. This is the "foot in the door" technique.

Cialdini reports on a study conducted in Bloomington, Indiana. Residents were asked to predict what they would say if they were asked to contribute three hours of their time to raise money for the American Cancer Society. Not wanting to come across as uncharitable, many people said they would. As a result of this simple procedure, the American Cancer Society experienced a 700 percent increase in the number of volunteers willing to help with fundraising. A simple verbal commitment can be a powerful thing.

Sometimes we make a mistake. Instead of making a second mistake in line with the first mistake, just to be consistent, it is much better to deal with the tension that the inconsistency created in the first place. Let's say you volunteered to serve on a committee at work. While volunteering is generally good, you are bombarded with work now and you just volunteered because you wanted to be nice to the person who invited you. Everybody at work says how helpful you are and what a good job you are doing in the committee. You feel pressured to stay on the committee for longer than you can realistically do it. Your other work and your personal life suffer because of your willingness to take on too many things.

Instead of staying on for a second term on the committee, which would be a mistake, you decide to assert yourself and say, "Thank you so much for inviting me. I really enjoyed my work with all of you on the committee to revise the purchasing guidelines, but at this time I cannot afford the time." You probably made a mistake saying yes the first time around, but it doesn't mean you have to keep saying yes. For the sake of consistency you risk making a second mistake. Remember, two wrongs don't make a right, even if the second wrong is consistent with the first one!

You can see this mistake in college students who don't want to change majors because they feel that they already invested one or two semesters in their initial choice. They feel committed, and to be consistent, they are willing to stick with a choice that ultimately is not good for them. In this case, it is better to stop being consistent and start being authentic, even if it takes you another semester to finish college. An extra semester of work is better than twenty years in a profession you dislike.

While commitment and consistency can be employed to manipulate you to do something you really don't want, they can also be used to get you to do things you do want. Committing to exercise with a friend three times a week is a good first step. Having a precise time and place to do so is even better. Committing to saving 10 percent of your salary can also improve your long-term financial well-being. Creating an automatic transfer from your paycheck to a savings account is even better than verbal assurances.

In addition to the *contrast*, *reciprocation*, and *commitment* mechanisms of influence, we are also highly susceptible to the principle of *social proof*. According to Cialdini, if other people approve of something or laugh at a joke, we are more likely to follow the herd and to laugh. This is very much in line with the principle of *conformity*. This is why marketers often say things like, "Ninety percent of people prefer our illustrious brand over the calamitous product put out by the competition."

As a mature reader you are probably thinking "this would never happen to me. I'm an independent thinker." All we can say is think again. There are disastrous behaviors such as smoking, drinking, eating junk food, and spending too much that you rationalize because "other people do it." We recently heard someone say that not having health insurance is not the end of the world because he knew so many people who went without health insurance. In Hebrew there is a saying: "Tzarat rabim nachamat tipshim," which means "The sorrow of many is the comfort of fools."

Having studied influence and persuasion for many years, in different settings, across various groups, Cialdini discovered that *liking*, *authority*, and *scarcity* also impact our thinking, feeling, and doing. We are more likely to follow advice of people we like and respect. We gravitate toward people who are warm, friendly, and attractive. Salespeople strive to find commonalities with shoppers to increase the likeability factor.

We like people who are like us. People in sales want to establish similarities between you and them. To accomplish that goal they will ask you where you are from, what high school you attended, and what TV programs you like; all in the hope of finding something in common.

During Donald Trump's presidential campaign he gave seventy zillion TV interviews. He often talked about *liking* people, how much people *like* him, and the fact that he is very *likeable*. It was all about *liking*. He also tried to establish his authority in certain fields, such as business and negotiation. Trump may not be an expert on many things, but his campaign got a lot of people to vote for him nonetheless.

Authority figures tend to influence our thinking and action. Unfortunately, some people overgeneralize from one area of expertise to another, leading to unknown consequences. Trump is thought to be an authority on negotiations. Many people really don't know how big of an authority he will turn out to be on foreign policy or health care, but in the eyes of many people it doesn't matter because he is a big authority on something many people like: money!

The psychological mechanism by which authority works is something like this: "This person is famous or important or highly respected, therefore I must pay attention to what she says." The problem with this logic is that sometimes the person is an authority on something completely unrelated to the issue at hand. Rationally, there is no reason to think that a famous athlete would be an expert on diarrhea, but you often see celebrities advertising things they have no clue about. They are paid big dollars because they are some kind of authority on something.

Scarcity is another powerful means of compliance. Ora and I pride ourselves on being ultrarational, calculated, measured, and frugal. However, all our rationality went out the window when we were trying to buy a new condo. The mere insinuation of another buyer putting an offer on the condo we liked was enough to suppress the last inch of equanimity in our mind.

As soon as we heard that another buyer might snatch the condo, we experienced a huge adrenaline rush. For all we know, the sellers may have completely fabricated the existence of a competitor, but in our minds, the idea of losing this unique and irreplaceable condo was unfathomable. Our two doctorates in psychology were no match for the surge of irrationality. The purchase ended up being a good one, but we probably paid more than we should have, thanks to the principle of scarcity.

As soon as we think that we are about to lose something, the motivation to get it is tripled. This is why car dealers advertise limited edition models and why stores put a time limit on sales. It is all to create a sense of scarcity and urgency. If you miss this vehicle or this sale you may never get the object of your desire.

Cialdini shares the story of his brother, who put himself through school by selling used cars privately. To generate a sense of scarcity and urgency, he would advertise used cars in the newspapers (this principle is so old that it worked even before the existence of the internet). People would call him on the phone and he would invite all prospective buyers to inspect the car *at the same time.*

As soon as the first interested party would open the hood, there would be five more waiting in line to kick the tires. That created a sense of scarcity that helped to sell the car really fast. The potential unavailability of a product creates a painful sense of loss, which, in turn, accelerates the desire to acquire it.

So far in the chapter you've learned about a number of important blatant and subtle cues that can influence your behavior. They come from *people*, *places*, and *things*. [11] What are some cues in your context and how are you responding to them? How do these cues influence how you're working toward your goal?

Think of cues that help you achieve your goal. Which people, places, and things can help you achieve your goal? We provide the first example, you do the rest.

- *Goal:* Eat healthier foods
- *Things*: Plenty of fruits and vegetables in visible places in my house
- *My reaction*: I tend to eat healthy snacks.
- *People*: My spouse rewards me for eating well
- *My reaction*: I feel proud and encouraged to keep going
- *Place*: My kitchen
- *My reaction*: Gravitate towards fruits and veggies

Your turn:

- *Goal:*
- *Things*:
- *My reaction*:
- *People*:

- *My reaction*:
- *Place*:
- *My reaction*:

Now let's do the following exercise for cues that get in the way of your goal.

- *Goal*: Improve my nutrition
- *Place*: Going to office parties after work where they don't serve healthy food
- *My reaction*: I tend to eat unhealthy snacks because I'm usually hungry after work
- *People*:
- *My reaction*:
- *Things*:
- *My reaction*:

Controlling our environment can go a long way in helping us behave in ways that are consistent with our goals. Nonetheless, not all cues to problem behavior are within our control. A colleague bringing a freshly baked cake to share can strain our effort to avoid sweets. An unexpected pop up on our computer advertising a sale can trigger spending. A particularly interesting TV program can thwart our plan to study. Now that you've learned about the impact of cues, let's see what we can do to change them.

Change the Cues

We can change our behavior by changing cues in the environment.[12] We can remove cues that tempt us to do things we don't want to do. We can also, in turn, introduce cues that will elicit behaviors consistent with our goals. As we discussed earlier, there are two main types: *blatant* and *subtle* cues. Within each of the two categories there are cues related to *people*, *places*, and *things*. We will see first how we can change the blatant cues.

Change Blatant Cues

Starting with people, let's go back to Ariely's experiment with masturbating male college students. Students predicted that when faced with a naked sexual partner, in the heat of the moment, they were less likely to practice safe sex. A naked body in front of you is a pretty blatant cue that something is going to happen. The cue in the form of sex with a stranger should automatically trigger a reminder to use a condom.

People constitute triggers for all kinds of healthy and unhealthy behaviors. If you want to increase your visits to the gym, it is good to make a commitment in public that you shall exercise three times a week with Steven. Commitments carry a lot of weight. When we feel obligated to a friend we are more likely to follow up on a promise. Ora and I have made a commitment to get up at 5:00 a.m. each morning to do some writing before I have to go to work. It works! I doubt that I could have gotten up so early by myself, but with help from Ora we have been on this routine for several months now.

There are ways in which individuals can make our lives miserable. A despotic boss, disrespectful professor, or controlling partner can cause a lot of damage. It is possible to be a positive, well-adjusted person who is in a bad relationship at work or at home. We need to be aware of the source of our misery. Sometimes, as Sartre said, "Hell is other people." It is advisable always to try and resolve conflict with a mix of assertiveness and empathy, but occasionally no amount of interpersonal acumen will do. In that case, you need to remove that person from your life, or you need to remove yourself from the situation. People can help one another, but they can also drive each other crazy.

Places like the kitchen, restaurants, or the outdoors can also be blatant cues. These are cues to prepare healthy meals, gorge on junk food, or exercise. The road is often a stressful cue, especially if you live in Miami and your name is Isaac. Here, you often encounter drivers who never signal, cross in red, swing back and forth across lanes, and never let you into their lane, no matter how politely you ask. They ignore helpful cues such as their signal stick, red traffic lights, and the most basic rules of courtesy. To cope with this stressful cue, we decided to change the cue.

When we moved to Miami ten years ago we decided to buy a house close to work to avoid the crazy drivers and the daily surge in cortisol that accompanies every commute. Ora insisted we buy close to campus for a couple of reasons. First, to make sure she could get to work independently in her wheelchair; and second, to prevent my premature death from stress or an accident. The location of our house is a major source of well-being. Avoiding Miami traffic and all the unhealthy cues associated with it is one of the best decisions we ever made.

We also made a decision to purchase a weekend condo on Hollywood Beach so that we can enjoy the outdoors. Friday is our cue to go to the beach and enjoy long walks by the ocean. We usually travel after rush hour, so we can enjoy a nice conversation during the forty-five-minute ride from Coral Gables to Hollywood. Spending weekends next to a beautiful boardwalk and a scenic view is a reminder to stop working on this book all the time and get out for a stroll.

Your office can be more or less conducive to work. If there is loud music playing and a pile of papers strewn all over your desk it may be really hard to concentrate. These are pretty obvious signs of disarray. If you want to encourage productivity, especially yours, start with a clean desk and a quiet place. If you want to be more efficient at work, the best thing you can do is to turn off your email alert so that emails don't distract you while you're concentrating. This is an example of changing the cues. Email alerts disrupt the flow of your thinking. They're distracting cues. By simply turning that off, you have made a significant change in your environment.

If you are trying to create a clean environment around you, it helps to infuse citrus smell in the air. Some air freshener can do miracles. In a couple of studies it was found that doctors tend to wash their hands more often before examining patients, and people tend to clean their tables more when there is citrus scent in the air. The scent is priming us to be clean. A smell is a thing that brings us to the third kind of blatant cues: light, smell, noise, words. Some blue lights tend to suppress melatonin, which helps us sleep, while soft lights help us fall asleep.

Passwords to our Amazon account, like the words "frugal" or "bankruptcy" can remind us to be thrifty when we're shopping online. The effect of priming is well established in psychology, and we can use this to good effect. A light, a smell, or a word can be our allies or our road to perdition. [13] The irresistible smell coming from Cinnabon bakeries can interfere with the best-laid plans for dieting. The sight of vodka during a cocktail party can ruin your seven-week sobriety spell. If you are trying to cut down on your liquor consumption, refraining from the sight of alcohol will help. If you are trying to eat better, or less, consider some of Wansink's suggestions:

• Use nine- to ten-inch plates at home
• Choose the small plate at buffets
• Limit trips to the buffet to just one
• Bring a healthy lunch to work to avoid going to the buffet
• Preselect restaurants with plenty of tasty and healthy items
• Remove lounge type chairs from the kitchen because they invite prolonged stays near food

- Remove the TV from the kitchen for same reason
- Place on the kitchen counter a bowl with at least two type of fruits
- Remove from the counter bread, chips, candy, cookies, snacks, and breakfast cereals
- Place precut fruit and veggies on the center shelf of the fridge
- Store veggie leftovers in clear containers
- Store nonvegetable leftovers in opaque containers
- Eat salads and vegetables first
- Use small serving bowls and spoons instead of tongs
- Place a glass of water in front of every plate at the dinner table
- Place fruits and vegetables at the front of the shopping cart at the supermarket
- Put less-healthy snacks in difficult to reach cupboards
- Put a refillable bottle of water next to your desk
- Remove candy bowl from your desk

You can tell yourself that you will work on your willpower, but it's so much easier and efficient to change the cues instead of changing your motivation [14] behaviors is about changing cues. As we understand this more and more, we can try to create situations where we're more likely to behave in desired ways and avoid situations where we're likely to behave in undesirable fashion.

This can be challenging sometimes because most of the time we're not in complete control of our environments. For instance, how many times have you tried to eat healthy foods when you go out to restaurants only to find the menu offerings are limited for you? How did it feel when you wanted to choose a healthy item from the menu but your choices were unhealthy?

If you are health conscious, you would have been frustrated. When most people find themselves in similar situations they go ahead and order bad food anyway because they are hungry. You may avoid this situation by going to restaurants that offer healthy items on the menu. If you change the context and the cues, like going to a different restaurant, you can achieve your goals much faster.

In addition to reading and changing cues in our environment, we also need to be prepared to respond to unexpected or subtle cues that threaten to thwart our goals. In other words, we have to take responsibility for how we respond to problem cues. When we cannot change triggers, we have to focus on how to best respond to them.

Let's practice with the following goal: "I want to avoid unhealthy foods and eat more healthy foods." I provide the first few examples and you do the rest.

Scenario #1:

- *Unhealthy cue*: Junk food at home
- *Ways to change the unhealthy cues*: Clear my house of junk food

Scenario #2:

- *Unhealthy cue*: Candy bowl at work desk
- *Ways to change the unhealthy cues*: Chuck the candy bowl

Scenario #3:

- *Unhealthy cue*: Vending machine on route to office
- *Ways to change the unhealthy cues*: Take a different route to avoid the cue

Scenario #4:

- *Unhealthy cue*: Hanging out with friends who eat junk food
- *Ways to change the unhealthy cues:* Ask friends not to tempt you

Scenario #5:

- *Unhealthy cue:* _____
- *Ways to change the unhealthy cues:*

_____

_____

_____

Scenario #6:

- *Unhealthy cue:* _____
- *Ways to change the unhealthy cues:*

_____

_____

_____

Change Subtle Cues

It is hard to change subtle cues because they are difficult to detect, but it is not impossible. Social norms tend to influence us in unconscious ways, as we saw in the Asch experiments. A culture of excessive eating and drinking is so pervasive that it is hard to step out of it. Yet, we are massively influenced by what most people around us do and feel. If we're encircled by healthy people, we tend to imitate their demeanor. If we're surrounded by slothful friends, we're unlikely to exercise. Our weight and our mood go up and down depending on the company we keep.

Similarly, our behavior is impacted by the places where we work, eat, and relax. Eating dinner with the TV on will guarantee that you eat more. An office with candy bowls on every desk will guarantee mindless consumption of sugar. These are subtle things, but when you add up the sugar of every piece of candy every day, times twenty days of work per month, times fifty-two weeks, you begin to see the cumulative impact of "just one piece."[15]

While these may be negative settings, there are positive places that can make us healthier. Exposure to nature has been shown to accelerate healing in patients after surgery.[16]

There are people, there are places, and then of course there are things that influence our behavior. Behavioral economists recommend setting defaults for things we want to achieve. Changing a cue from effortful to automatic is a step in the right direction. If you wish to save more, arrange to have an automatic deduction from your paycheck every month. If you want to join a pension plan, have companies set up an opt-out as opposed to an opt-in procedure.

Defaults are the automatic option. If you join a new company, and there is an opt-in option for joining the pension plan, you are less likely to do it than if there is an opt-out system. In other words, places of employment where joining the pension plan is automatic enlist more staff. In contrast, places where the employee has to fill out a form to join do not enlist as many. Defaults are important also in organ donation. States where drivers have to opt-out of the plan enroll many more donors. When donations are the automatic option, more drivers join the plan.[17]

At home, my default is to exercise every day for an hour before I go to work. This is my automatic schedule. If I have to go to work very early for a meeting, then I might have to vary my routine once, but I don't have to reinvent my schedule every day, which would be tedious. If I have to reprioritize my day every day, exercising would become a low priority after finishing this book and answering ninety-seven emails from the night before. Defaults make life easier, which is what we need to create a healthier lifestyle.

When we go out to eat, our default is to go to restaurants that cater to vegans. We have a list of about fifteen restaurants in Miami that serve delicious vegan meals. We have narrowed down the list of eateries from hundreds to a handful. We get some variety, but we still eat healthy meals, which is what we prefer.

Making decisions, following up on them, and remembering to perform an action every month can be tiresome. It is much easier to put things on automatic pilot. Ora and I have had credit cards for thirty-five years. We never miss a bill, or pay less than the full amount, because our credit card is on automatic payment. Defaults are about going with the flow. They require little effort and attention, which is why we're more likely to stick with them.

Life is so complicated and we all have so many things competing for our attention that we are likely to forget things or to postpone them. Defaults simplify life. It is the difference between having a method and having to invent one every month or every day. Instead of making decisions when to pay bills, go to the gym, or to call your parents, you have a set time for these things.

When it comes to finishing projects and procrastination, a study found that having firm deadlines helps with the quality of the project and the timeliness of submission. It is all about planning in advance.[18] Reminders and plans are little nudges to get you to do something you want to do, or that is good for you. Students at Yale University were encouraged to get the flu shot. Some were told to get it. Others were told exactly where to go and when to get it and were given a map of the student health center.

The second group was nudged more than the first one. The helpful cues, like the map, nudged the students to check this off their list of things to do. Compared to the first, many more students in the second group complied with the request to get the shot.[19] Little things like Post-It notes and maps can help you get things done.

From eating to saving to procrastinating, there are little things you can do to set cues that will nudge you in the right direction. You have to keep in mind that some cues are easier to detect than others. A pack of cigarettes is a pretty easy cue to spot, but the opinion of your friends is a subtle cue that often goes undetected. Yet, their views on what is proper and normal and acceptable may have a big impact on you, regardless of the merit of their position.

It is important to note, however, that in the Asch experiments not all participants acquiesced to the view of the majority. Some people stuck to their perceptions despite what everybody else said. We might say that these participants read the cues that social norms may be wrong. Knowing that group pressure exists, that the bystander effect is real, and that we tend to stick to things we committed to, regardless of their merit, can help us move in a new direction. We have to master the art of reading cues and changing cues. Some cues come in the form of a scent, and some in the form of a map. In different ways, they all shape our behavior in conscious and unconscious ways. The best medicine to cure cluelessness is to read the cues and change the cues.

THE LAUGHING SIDE

The C in I CAN stands for "context." What is happening in your surroundings? What is going on around you? What do you see? What do you hear? This is all part of context. Surroundings impact your health and well-being. If there is a lot of pollution in the environment you will have a hard time breathing. If everybody around you drinks in excess, eats in excess, and smokes in excess, hurry up and get one of those "no medical exam required" life insurance policies on their behalf. You will become rich quickly. It's like derivatives and credit swaps on slothful people.

To create a healthy environment in our house, we don't bring into it any toxic substances. That is why our cupboards are empty and we're very skinny. When we feel the urge to eat we count to three, pretend it is Yom Kippur, and faint.

It's all about the cues. To overcome temptations, we need to control cues in the environment. If every time you open the pantry there are ten bags of potato chips jumping at you, you will pay attention to them. If every time you open the fridge there are seven slices of cold pizza, you *will eat them*. Controlling cues is the key. Research shows that children choose more fruits and veggies in school when they're arranged at eye level in the cafeteria.

This is why they're never at eye level. Instead, schools are getting sponsorships from the makers of sodas, sugary foods, and the corn syrup fraternity to put all their products at eye level. To assuage their conscience, the food and drink giants buy the school three new basketballs every semester.

The Meaning of Sexy

In our cultural context, sexy has a very narrow definition, which means that 6.916 billion people, and most importantly I (Isaac), have no chance to appear on the cover of *People* magazine. However, for those of us who don't fit the narrow definition of sexy, I have good news. Sexy doesn't have to refer just to the carnal domain. Sexy can be a metaphor for appealing, exciting, desirable, attractive, educated, wise, fair, interesting, and stimulating.

I'm aware that this theory may well be perceived as an apologia for my big ears, but I trust the reader will see beyond them. I'm also aware that my argument may grow out of my charming personality, but I hope you will not get distracted by it.

In our culture, we all want to be physically attractive. Women spend billions of dollars on cosmetics, plastic surgery, clothes, and colonic cleansing just to be beautiful and sexy, on the outside and the inside. They spend inordinate amounts of money on nail salons. Men go to gyms and buy supplements to build muscle. They color their hair to look their best. Some even shave their chests. Many go to tan salons to look gorgeous while they fry their brains and acquire new kinds of skin cancer.

We spend countless hours in front of the mirror, just to look right. I get that. We want to be striking. We want to feel good about ourselves and we want to impress others. It is just human nature to conquer the object of our sexual desire as it is to run through red lights in Miami.

But this conception of sexy is way too narrow. Instead of this constricted definition, I embrace a comprehensive meaning that implies *likeable, striking, clever, titillating, well-educated*, and *cultured*. When you think about sexy in these terms, there are countless possibilities to increase our beauty quotient: you can buy a fake Ph.D., read the *New York Times* book reviews and pretend that you have read the entire book, and use foreign words nobody understands, including you.

Unfortunately, we often focus strictly on erotic sexiness, at the expense of psychological or interpersonal charm. My aim is to cultivate a wider array of attractive features that (a) go beyond physical allure and (b) distract people from looking at my ears.

Let's face it, not all of us are Hugh Jackman. But fortunately, some of us have delightful personalities. We might as well build on what we have, or can nurture. Short of plastic surgery, not much I can do about my big ears, but I can nurture my work ethic, psychological wisdom, and cultural sophistry, to say nothing of my interpersonal magnetism. If you do that, you have a higher chance of having your tweets read by women; especially those who have not seen your picture yet.

My definition of sexy is liberating because it gives you so many ways to be attractive and so many ways to work on it. Unlike our genetic splendor, we can refine our wisdom, virtues, and self-esteem. We can go to workshops that charge $5,000 per day so that somebody can tell you that you're a worthy person. Alternatively, you can get a fake degree from one of the many fake colleges that are desperate to increase their graduation rate.

We can even improve our physical well-being, regardless of the features we inherited. Take me, for example. My cardiovascular age is exactly half of my chronological age, but you don't see many women coming to congratulate me for this feat. I wonder what would happen if I walk around with a sign describing my education, physical fitness scores, scholarly awards, and a short version of my resume. For one, they wouldn't be looking at my ears. Best case scenario, they may not even realize I have a flat gluteus maximus. As a matter of fact, and this is totally patentable, an entrepreneur can design custom made t-shirts with noticeable aspects of your biography. These are some of the fascinating aspects of my personal profile that would make for a super-cool t-shirt:

- Page views of my blog by Android users: 377 (2 percent)
- Google Scholar i10-index: 78
- Blog views from Ukraine: 358
- VO2Max: 42.3 ml/kg/min
- IQ: undetectable
- Body Fat: 10 percent
- GRE: repressed
- BMI: 18
- Metabolic Score: 95
- GPA in first year college: classified
- Google Scholar h-index: 38
- Citations: 7235
- TMI

I may not have perfect facial features, to say nothing of my girly voice and graying hair, but I can perfect other aspects of body and soul, such as the ability to come up with innumerable excuses for my horrible physiognomy.

The obsession with sex is not surprising though. It is the perfect storm. Businesses market seductive products. We crave attention. We think that looking sexy will make us stand out.

Standing out among a crowd feeds our hunger for attention. Your Google Scholar h-index goes up. We're rewarded with praise.

We think of sex as a shortcut to mattering, but authentic mattering is so much more than erotic encounters. Mattering is also about being appreciated for virtuous, kind, and ethical behavior, and being loved by your wife despite a barely noticeable gluteus maximus.

Unless we cultivate other qualities, popular culture will continue to foment the cult of sex and narcissism. Unless we nourish our spiritual and relational beings, we will remain fixated on erotic attraction, self-absorption, and selfies. But until we reach such an evolved cultural stage, there are a number of things we can do:

1. *Trigger alert I:* Every time people are going to talk about someone *attractive* and remind me of my imperfections, I want them to let me know in advance so that I can decide whether to participate in the conversation or not.
2. *Trigger alert II:* Every time people are going to talk about someone *unattractive* and remind me of my imperfections, I want them to let me know in advance so that I can crawl under a table in fetal position.
3. *Safe area I:* Whenever other people are talking about someone *attractive* I want to go to a safe zone and play with stuffed animals.
4. *Safe area II:* Whenever other people are talking about someone *unattractive*, I can hug Dumbo.
5. *Safe area III:* I can go to a waxing salon and remove these annoying pieces of hair sticking out of my right ear.

Context Is Everything

The biggest lesson in well-being is knowing what surroundings are good for you and which ones cause convulsions. In my case, shopping induces not just convulsions, but also STS (sudden Trump syndrome), which includes temper tantrums and involuntary repetitions of the word *disaster.* That is nothing compared to the pain and suffering I inflict on my wife.

My congenial personality changes dramatically the minute we set foot in a store. Precipitously, my affable self becomes grouchy and grumpy. In the best of times, I manage to laugh at shoppers. In the worst of times, I get dizzy and swear irrepressibly in four languages.

Nevertheless, in my never-ending pursuit of (a) becoming a better husband and (b) overcoming my shopping phobia, I conducted a comparative study. I wanted to see if my mood would be better in certain shopping environs. The research consisted of comparing my mood while shopping for home goods at IKEA and JC Penny.

I was excited to go to IKEA because I admire the Swedes. I owned two Volvos, I respect their progressive social policies, and I value their egalitarian culture. My love for the Swedes was supposed to counteract the phobic aspects of shopping.

I was ready to begin the desensitization process. Unfortunately, to get to the local IKEA we had to contend with Miami traffic. It took us over an hour to get there. Once we arrived, we realized the store was the size of Aventura and Dolphin malls combined. If you're not from Miami, let me put it in context. IKEA is double the size of the former Yugoslavia.

After we parked our car we had to take three elevators to get to the right floor for the official start line. IKEA is not like any other store where you can roam around freely. In IKEA you must follow a single path and go through multiple sections en route to your destination. Before we got to ours, the kitchen section, we passed seventeen different departments enticing you to buy things that (a) you don't need, (b) will take you the entire weekend to assemble, and (c) will require that you spend the rest of the week cutting the carton boxes into small pieces that can fit into the recycling bin (the alternative is to throw the boxes in the garbage, contribute to global warming, and accelerate the submersion of Miami, not to mention environmental guilt and the looks of your green neighbors).

The traffic on the road was nothing compared to the foot traffic in the store. After thirty minutes of following signs and getting hit by baby strollers, we reached our destination. Ora got really excited. She inspected every single kitchen cabinet on display; opened every single drawer; compared hinges, colors, materials, design, door knobs, make, weight, and birth certificate of each countertop. All combined, there were 65,389 possible combinations of color, style, design, material, and blood type of kitchen cabinets. Ora, of course, had to contemplate them all.

By the time Ora chose something she liked, I was comatose, but we were finally ready to approach the friendly salesperson. I could tolerate the bombardment of stimulation in the expectation that, when ready, an efficient customer representative would give us the Swedish treatment.

As soon as Ora started explaining what she liked, the friendly salesperson directed us to a computer terminal, asked us to set up a password (what the *&$! ???), and basically told us *good luck*! It was up to us to figure out the pricing by inputting the size, make, color, wood type, and environmental footprint of each cabinet, door, and knob. Once you inserted the exact measures, height, width, race, ethnic origin, and sexual orientation of the cabinet, the computer would spit out an Excel spreadsheet with 95 lines and 543 rows with potential pricing options.

Once you figured out pricing, you had to press on a link that took you to a different portal. There you could enter all your biographical and logistical data, including address, door width, house type, pet names, country of origin, preferred language, and date of last colonoscopy. If you survived the screening, you could approach a customer service representative who would ask you to call a warehouse to see if your choice was available. At that point, I decided that the Swedes had gone completely mad with the *do it yourself* concept.

But wait, if you thought that this experience was not nightmarish enough, trying to get out of IKEA was a Kafkaesque ordeal. To get to the exit, you had to traverse the length and width of the store, twice, just to make sure that you saw all the wonderful things on sale.

If by the time I got to the store I was mildly neurotic, by the time I got out of it I was severely claustrophobic, agoraphobic, and Swedophobic. It turns out IKEA forces you to go through a labyrinth before you can see the exit sign. You cannot exit the store without going through twenty different sections tempting you to buy useless things that you have no idea how to assemble.

After the Swedish saga, we went to the JC Penny Home Goods store in Kendall. By the time we got there, Ora had already checked online three different types of sofas we were interested in. The friendly salesperson greeted us with a big smile. The store was nearly empty. It took us five seconds to get to the right section of the store and another three minutes to choose the right sofa, a matching La-Z-Boy, and a coffee table.

Compared to the IKEA torment, I felt jubilant. For starters, I could see the exit sign. There weren't 25,678 types of sofas, and most of all, I did not have to create a stupid password to buy what I wanted. From now on, I buy everything at JC Penny Home Goods, from sofas to broccoli to suppositories. If I cannot find it at JC Penny, I don't need it. Context is everything.

How to Fix Education

If you follow the tenet of *awareness*, to change something, you need to know the issue. For example, if you want to improve education, you'd expect politicians to know the first thing about it, unless your name is Betsy DeVos, and you happen to be the secretary of education in the United States.

Gazillion dollars have been invested in education reform recently. It is time to conduct an evaluation of these efforts to help DeVos. The most intelligent reform is the improvement of teacher evaluations according to a sophisticated statistical model called Value Added. According to the *Miami Herald*, this brilliant idea resulted in Julie Rich—Miami–Dade County Science Teacher of the Year—getting a poor evaluation because her students showed poor performance—in reading—a subject she never taught.

But wait, there is more. In Florida, many teachers were being evaluated on the performance of students they never even met. After a collective *oops* in Tallahassee, legislators changed the law last year to make sure that the evaluation was based on the achievement of students that teachers actually taught. When criticized for this mistake, legislators said in their defense that they cannot be expected to understand the bills they're voting on because they're the product of the failed education system in Florida. "We all grew up in Florida. How can we be expected to understand what we're reading when reading scores in Florida have been so low for so long?" asked a spokeswoman for the legislators.

In an effort to rectify this untenable situation, the Florida legislature is recruiting candidates from Massachusetts, the state with the best educational achievements in the country, which brings me to the recent PISA results.

When the Program for International Student Assessment, or PISA, released its 2013 results, which are supposed to show how recent educational reform efforts are working, there were a few surprises. *Education Week* published a summary of the outcomes on its December 3, 2013 edition. While the performance of US students in math, reading, and science remained stagnant since 2009, many other superpowers, such as Vietnam and Estonia, surpassed us. These two countries surpassed by far the United States in the 2015 PISA evaluation as well.

This unprecedented turn of events led the Obama administration to consider a second Vietnam invasion. "This is our opportunity to heal a national wound," said a spokesman for the president. A person close to the president told our sources that the invasion would have two specific goals: divert attention from the failed launch of HealthCare.gov and prepare the ground to send to Vietnam our failing students.

Dejected, some educational reformers are thinking of drastic measures, such as not allowing children with poor performance into public schools. "It is time we learned from Shanghai," said the chair of the National Council for the Destruction of Public Education (NCDPE). "In Shanghai, only the best get into public schools. It is time we rethought our strategy of decimating public education. In Shanghai, they allow into public schools only the most talented students. We can do the same in America.

"Many charter schools already screen out poor performers. It is about time all schools did the same. Our scores will go through the roof," she said. The chair of the bipartisan NCDPE held secret talks with Democrats and Republicans to plan next steps. All agreed on a plan to allow into public schools only gifted and talented students and to send to Vietnam all students with an IQ below 120. The Gates Foundation, which is frustrated with the slow pace of educational reform, will underwrite the Vietnam project. "Besides," said Melinda Gates, "We have a lot of experience in developing countries."

Richelle Mhee, founder of the organization Mhee First, added her voice to the chorus of praise for Eastern systems of education. "Over there," she said, "people don't come up with silly excuses such as poverty. It is school or homework 24/7/365; none of this mushy stuff about student mental health. Look at Mhee, I'm a product of that system, and I'm smart, productive, accomplished, and totally insensitive to human needs, the picture of perfection."

To make some sense of the whole education reform mess, I consulted with one of my colleagues, Professor Newt Rall, from the University of Objek Teef. Excerpts from our dialogue:

Isaac: Why is the United States falling behind in reading, science, and math?

Newt Rall: The United States has a much higher rate of poverty and inequality than other OECD countries. Poverty accounts for a great deal of educational failure in this country. Children from affluent communities or private schools in the United States do very well in international rankings.

Isaac: Then why don't we report just the results for rich children? It would be cheaper than sending most kids to Vietnam.

Newt Rall: That would be unethical.

Isaac: OK, Mr. Ethical, I can tell you're not from Miami. So why is there so much poverty in the United States?

Newt Rall: Without poor children, there wouldn't be employment opportunities for all the people telling the poor how to get out of poverty.

Isaac: I hear that when community schools fail to make progress the government shuts them down. When investment banks fail and send millions of people bankrupt, the government bails them out. Why is that?

Newt Rall: The government is afraid that investment bankers will go into teaching.

Isaac: The government just cut food stamps. Did they do that to teach poor children resilience?

Newt Rall: I don't think so.

Isaac: If another country deprived our children of food, would we invade that country?

Newt Rall: Probably.

Isaac: Preventable medical errors account for about 98,000 deaths per year. Should doctors be fired like teachers and hospitals shut down like poor performing schools?

Newt Rall: You should ask Trump.

Isaac: I hear Finland has one of the best education systems in the world. I hear they pay teachers well, teachers are highly respected, have time to prepare lessons and learn from one another. Also, I hear they don't test kids to death. Why don't we copy what they do?

Newt Rall: It wouldn't work here.

Isaac: Why?

Newt Rall: Because our teachers don't speak Finnish.

Isaac: I hear Finland is also a very egalitarian country. Why don't we try that?

Newt Rall: Because we would have to fire a lot of people telling the poor how to stop being poor, generating unemployment among highly paid consultants. Their egos couldn't handle that.

Isaac: I hear that a lot of these new teachers without clinical experience don't last more than two years. Why is that?

Newt Rall: Because after two years they become consultants.

Isaac: Is teacher bashing working in improving education?

Newt Rall: No.

Isaac: Perhaps they're not bashing them hard enough.

Newt Rall: Oh no, they're bashing them hard, alright.

Isaac: Who is next?

Newt Rall: My sources tell me they're going after parents, deans of schools of education, professors of education, and the president of Estonia for giving our reforms a bad name.

Isaac: I just attended an educational policy conference where I heard that the key to educational success is for all the states to adopt the common core standards, tell liberals to stop whining about poverty, use homelessness as a bonding experience for the entire family, replace all public schools with for profit charter schools, determine teacher pay on the ability of other teachers to learn from Enron, and send 28 million children from the United States to South Korea to learn discipline. Do you agree?

Newt Rall: You said a lot of things. Can you be more specific?

Isaac: Oh academics! Never mind. I hear the results of the new National Assessment of Educational Progress show that there is a constant improvement in reading and math for white, African American, Asian, and Hispanic children. If that is the case, why do so many reformers say the opposite?

Newt Rall: If you have good PR, the truth is irrelevant. Betsy DeVos knows a lot about PR.

Isaac: If minorities are not advancing fast enough to close the achievement gap, can we give rich kids a break for two years until other kids catch up?

Newt Rall: That hasn't been tried before.

Isaac: Can we blame the educational problems of our country on the Russia investigation into collusion with the Trump campaign?

Newt Rall: Trump hasn't tried that before, either.

Isaac: What has been tried then?

Newt Rall: A hodgepodge of charter schools, testing, more testing, deprofessionalization of the teaching profession along with calls for more highly qualified teachers, turn around consultants, and no teacher left unbashed.

Isaac: Have these strategies been subjected to rigorous longitudinal randomized controlled trials?

Newt Rall: Yes, Finland is the experimental condition and we're the comparison group.

Isaac: So who won?

Newt Rall: Finland.

Isaac: So why are we not invading Finland?

Newt Rall: The president is busy criticizing the media for our educational failure and everything else in the world.

Chapter Five

Mastering a Plan to Make It Stick

THE LEARNING SIDE

This is the time to design your plan of action. For every goal you set for yourself there must be a plan to go along with it.[1] As the last driver of change, it is only appropriate that we learn how to make a plan, and more importantly, how to make it stick. Make a plan and make it stick.

Make a Plan

We experience well-being when we're able to achieve important goals that we set for ourselves. Learn how to make a plan that is consistent with your values and priorities. Then *grease* the plan and get into action! GREASE is a plan of action consisting of six simple principles: *gradual, reinforced, easy, alternatives, supported,* and *educated.* But before we get there, let's do a thought experiment.

Imagine Your Best Possible Self

Think about yourself in the future. Imagine that your life has gone as well as it could. You have worked hard and managed to accomplish your most important goals. Now write about what you have imagined.

_____

_____

_____

_____

_____

A version of this exercise was originally designed by Professor Laura King from the University of Missouri Columbia.[2] A number of studies have found that engaging in this exercise for twenty minutes over a course of a few days resulted in higher levels of reported happiness. According to Professor Sonja Lyubomirsky,[3] it can also help establish the connection between present day actions and long-term goals. It can inform the goals you need to work on today in order to realize your dreams and aspirations tomorrow. Which goals would you need to accomplish in your present life in order to reach your long-term aspirations?

Gradual

Take small steps at first.[4] Don't run before you walk. Avoid shocking your system with drastic changes that are not sustainable. For example, if you haven't exercised in a long time, start with walking twenty minutes a day instead of running for forty-five. You can then add a few minutes here and there until you start running. If you want to get up earlier, don't go from 7 a.m. to 5 a.m. Give your body a chance to get used to the new routine slowly.

Reinforced

Which rewards work for you? How can you reinforce yourself for making progress toward your goal? Reinforcements come in all sorts of ways. You can tell yourself that you've accomplished something important, you can take yourself to the movies, or you can share the news in social media to get reinforcement from friends and family. Writing down your accomplishments in a diary is also a good idea. Telling yourself that you are getting closer to becoming the person you want to be is a positive reinforcement.

Easy

Since changing a behavior can be difficult, do whatever you can to make it easier. Self-efficacy is built on small successes. If you're studying another language, set an easy goal for the first week, like studying twenty minutes three times a week. Be sure the goal is realistic. If twenty minutes three times a week is too much, start with twice a week.

Make it easier by eliminating cues for problem behavior and introducing cues for healthy behavior. Whatever you do, don't tempt yourself.

What can you do to make it easier for yourself to meet your goal? What small steps can you take in order to be successful and build self-efficacy? Which cues in your environment do you need to change?

Alternatives

Find substitutes for the behavior you want to change.[5] If you like sweets, but you need to lower your sugar consumption, how about eating fruit instead? If you want to become vegetarian but worry about lack of protein, make sure you get enough from legumes, nuts, and whole grains. If you're stuck in a pattern of bickering with your kids every morning because you leave the house for school late, how about setting the alarm to go off twenty minutes earlier? If you experience boredom, how about picking up a hobby like playing an instrument or gardening?

What are some alternatives that can help you achieve your goal?

Supported

Get help from friends and family. Make a commitment to a friend or relative that you're serious about changing an aspect of your life, like improving your diet, and ask them to support you. Create a team of supporters around you. Change is a team sport; it requires the support of others who celebrate your accomplishments, and lift you up when you're down.

Who can you count on to support your goal? What do you need from whom in order to achieve your goal?

Educated

Inform yourself about the issue you're dealing with. If you want to quit smoking, learn about alternatives. Don't go from cigarettes to e-cigarettes just because they're advertised as a safe form of smoking. If you want to lose weight, don't go on a crazy diet that doesn't work. Instead, get started on a lifestyle that balances healthy eating with proper physical activity. Generally, products that offer great promises tend to exaggerate their claims.

Have you ever seen the commercials that list the possible side effects of medications? These can be serious, so don't ignore them. Be an informed consumer. Spend some time asking experts or reading on the issue before you jump from one problem to the next. The good news is that many problems can be alleviated in natural ways. Identify a person you respect or a website from a reliable organization and consult with them. Get good sources from the library and read up on the issue. People who have managed to change the behavior you're after are usually good sources of information.

Who can you consult with about the issues you're facing?

Make It Stick

We all know how tempting it can be to return to a problem behavior. There are various things you can do to fortify yourself and help you stick with your goal. Consider the following:

- In the early stage of change, avoid people, places, and things that are triggers for problem behavior.
- Remind yourself of your long-term goal and the benefits that will accrue from achieving it.
- Tell yourself that you have self-discipline and can withstand temptations.
- Distract yourself by doing something that will take your mind off the urge to indulge.
- If you unexpectedly find yourself in a tempting situation, go somewhere else if possible.
- Reach out to a loved one or a close friend who can help you resist the urge.
- Use a plan that you have prepared in advance in order to prevent a potential slip.
- Keep monitoring and recording your behavior. Record even if you slip.
- Continue to reinforce desirable behavior. Come up with different rewards to keep it fresh.
- If you have a strong craving, imagine that it is an ocean wave that you can ride. It will eventually pass.

Surfing the urge is a mindfulness-based technique developed by Alan Marlatt for dealing with addictions.[6] It was used in one study to help long-time smokers deal with an intense urge to indulge their habit. Smokers learned to mindfully attend to their craving in a compassionate and nonjudgmental manner. They envisioned their craving as an ocean wave that strengthens, crests, and ultimately subsides. Rather than resisting their craving or trying to suppress it, they envisioned surfing it, much like a surfer catching a ride on a wave.

If you experience a strong craving to engage in a habit you're trying to change, you can try this technique. Remind yourself that a craving will peak like a wave but will ultimately pass. See if you can adopt a curious attitude toward your craving. What sensations do you feel in your body? What thoughts are going through your mind? Imagine yourself as a surfer, riding a high wave. Stay on top of the wave until it dissolves.

Practice Saying No

Other people can encourage and support our goal but they can also interfere with our plans, at times unknowingly.[7] A colleague bringing a home-baked dessert to share or a friend who wants to meet up at a bar are some examples. If meeting an old friend at a bar will risk a return to drinking behavior, suggest another location. If your dessert-bearing colleague is a good friend, ask the person not to tempt you. You can also envision the offer of the yummy dessert and practice saying no.

Does sticking to your goal require saying no to someone? What do you need to say to whom in order to persevere with your goal and make it stick? What would you gain by expressing what you need? What reactions do you anticipate?

Envision a conversation that would help you stick with your goal. Practice what you would say and how the other person may react. Envision a positive outcome that would further your goal.

Plan Ahead

Planning ahead for high-risk situations can go a long way.[8] It is not always possible or even desirable to avoid all people, places, or things associated with the behavior you want to change.

Watson and Tharp suggest making "if-then" plans to help deal with barriers.[9] By trying to foresee situations that may thwart your goal, you can develop a plan for dealing with them.

How can you plan for high risk situations that may interfere with your goal? What rules can you make for yourself to help you navigate this situation?

Don't Let a Slip Be Your Downfall

We're often disheartened when we resolve to change something but slip. The reality is that when we try to change a problem behavior, slips are the norm rather than the exception. So rather than chastising yourself for having a setback, tell yourself that a slip is no reason to give up.[10] Most people who are ultimately successful experience a slip or two along the way.

The thing to do is to get up, dust yourself off, and get back on the horse. In fact, your slip can be an important source of information, a way of learning about yourself. You can regard the slip as a learning opportunity. Remind yourself that slips are normal, expected, and a part of life.

Risks, Opportunities, Weaknesses, and Strengths

To make a plan and to make it stick it helps to understand the factors that might facilitate or inhibit change. Risks and weaknesses may hinder change while opportunities and strengths may enable transformation. Together, risks, opportunities, weaknesses, and strengths form the acronym ROWS. We will call them ROWS for change.

Risks and opportunities pertain to external factors, such as a new job or moving to a new neighborhood. Weaknesses and strengths refer to personal factors, such as lack of assertiveness or artistic ability. A risk to your personal well-being may be related to conflict with your boss. Poor relationships in general are a threat to happiness. Moving to a welcoming community with lots of green spaces and low crime may be an opportunity to go out and exercise more. Submitting an application for a new job may be an opportunity for self-actualization and better pay.

Empathy and hard work may be strengths of yours, but a tendency to say yes and to please everybody may be a weakness. We all have strengths and weaknesses, and we all face risks and opportunities in life.[11]

Find Your Stage of Change

Now that we are aware of our ROWS, we should ask ourselves what action to take now. Since each individual is in a different stage of personal development, you should identify in which stage of change you are right now. There are five options:

1. I never thought about doing something about it (precontemplation)
2. I'm thinking about doing something about it (contemplation)
3. I'm prepared to do something about it (preparation)
4. I'm doing something about it (action)
5. I've been doing something about it for some time (maintenance)

The five options correspond to five stages of change in the Transtheoretical Model (TTM) of change developed by Prochaska, Norcross, and DiClemente: Precontemplation, contemplation, preparation, action, and maintenance.[12] This model is very helpful in conceptualizing the next steps you need to take to move forward in your personal journey.

Once you've identified a goal to work on, you can select strategies that can help you in each stage of change. For example, if you're in precontemplation, you may need to raise awareness about an issue affecting your life. If you drink alcohol in excess but are clueless about the impact of your drinking on your family, you may need to increase your *awareness*. If you're already in the action stage, using *rewards* to sustain the new habit is a good idea. In this case, we can *create positive habits* by *rewarding* desired actions. If you're in the preparation stage, *connecting* with others and *communicating* your intent to eat better to your family and friends would help. Finally, to make your positive changes last, you need to *read the cues* and *change the cues* in the context of your life.

The objective is to move from precontemplation all the way to maintenance. In most cases, it would not be advisable to jump from contemplation to action without proper preparation. Lack of readiness can set you back. It is extremely important to anticipate barriers and have a plan to deal with them. If you plan to go for a walk after work, but your colleague always pulls you in at the last minute to ask for advice, you need to plan an appropriate response such as, "Rhonda, I would love to help you, but I'm in a rush. I'd be happy to help you with this report as soon as I come to the office tomorrow morning." Unless we plan for barriers, our best intentions can never materialized.

Remember to create "if-then" plans. If I plan to go for a walk right after work, but Rhonda is in the habit of asking me for help always at the last minute, I can anticipate that. One option might be to go to her desk around 3:00 p.m. and tell her that if she will need help from you it would be great to know by 4:00 p.m., as opposed to 5:29 p.m. Anticipating cues (Rhonda's request for last minute help) is helpful in devising a plan. Once you reach your goal (going for a walk after work every day), it is crucial to make it sustainable. Reinforcements can make this new behavior last.

Now that you know the essential drivers of change, and their associated skills, you can leverage them to help you move from one stage of change to the next. To understand better what skills might help at which point, let's explore the stages of change a little further.

Precontemplation If you don't acknowledge that you have a problem, offering you solutions is not going to help. This is not uncommon in cases of alcoholics who vehemently deny that they have a problem. They swear that they can control their drinking. A state of denial is a clear sign that you are not even contemplating taking action. This is why this stage is called precontemplation.

You may have thought of changing at some point but given up because it was just too hard. Quitting smoking is hard and exercising is hard, so why bother? Besides, you might say, "Health is all about genetics," so what's the point? Excuses such as these are common in people who have no intention of changing harmful habits. Another common refrain is that "we all die in the end." Some skills a person in precontemplation might use include: [13]

- *Challenge negative assumptions*: We might have had a negative experience trying to change something about our lives, and in all likelihood we are overgeneralizing. This overgeneralization leads us to think that we will never change or that it is pointless to try. We can challenge this negative assumption by focusing on past efforts where we did succeed.
- *Write a new story*: We can create a vision of our better selves in the future. Past is not destiny. We can identify pockets of meaning and accomplishments and build on that. We can press the pause button and reflect on what is really meaningful and valuable in life and reassess our habits accordingly.
- *Know yourself:* Evaluate your life and ask yourself if you are leading a meaningful and happy life. Do you have purpose in your life, or is it all about indulgence? How do you feel after binge drinking?
- *Know the issue*: Learning about alcoholism and addictions might help. Knowing their effect on other people is also important. Some alcoholics do not change until they see how their addictions are destroying their families. Remember that the second E in GREASE is for "educated."

Contemplation   This is the time when you start thinking that perhaps a change is in order. You realized that drinking or smoking or spending is an issue for you. Perhaps you are coming to terms with the fact that there is too much stress in your life. Possibly you realized that your relationship with your boyfriend is not going well or that this job is not the right fit for you. Maybe you've discovered that you're deriving neither pleasure nor purpose from your job. It may be time for a change. These contemplations may be helped by some of the following skills.

- *Set a goal:* If you are getting serious about changing jobs, taking guitar lessons, or quitting smoking, it is time to set a SMART goal. It is also important to anticipate barriers and to create concrete implementation plans.
- *Cope with negative emotions:* Emotions and feelings are talking to you all the time. If stress at work is making you miserable, don't ignore that feeling. Don't miss an opportunity to get in touch with your feelings and understand what they're telling you. One way to cope with negative emotions is to create a plan of action.
- *Read the cues:* If you're irritated with your kids, feeling depressed, and have missed deadlines at work, pay attention to these cues. What are these feelings and experiences telling you? It is usually one or both of the following: you're unhappy or unfulfilled.

Preparation   This is a crucial step in the process of change. You're getting ready to take action. Perhaps you're checking out gyms to get a membership, or you're reading books about a healthy lifestyle. You may be looking at courses online to get a graduate degree. You are warming up to the idea of a new behavior and a new lifestyle. Some strategies can help to maximize the preparation stage:

- *Collect positive emotions:* Celebrate the new decision you have made to improve an aspect of your life. Set a date to start going to the gym and get a new pair of runners. If you're about to start eating more fruits and vegetables, go to a local market and enjoy the colors and smells. Come home and bite into your favorite fruit. Make it a treat.
- *Communicate:* Tell your friends about your decision to volunteer at a youth center. Ask a buddy to go with you. Make a commitment that the two of you will join Big Brothers. Sharing with friends and family your resolution is likely to increase follow through, if for no other reason than to be consistent with our commitments.
- *Read cues:* Try to anticipate barriers. If you have to change the day you visit your grandmother, make sure you can see her some other time that doesn't conflict with your Big Sisters commitment. Plan accordingly.

Action   The day has come. You're volunteering at the youth center, eating more fruits and vegetables, walking twenty minutes a day, reading more, or taking a course online. Now that you've come thus far, you want to make sure your new behavior is consistent. Consider some of these strategies:

- *Create a positive habit:* Habits are reinforced through rewards. Rewards come in different shapes and forms depending on your taste. Phoning a friend to tell her that you've started volunteering can be a nice reward. Watching your favorite TV program works for some people. Writing on your Facebook page about it is another form. You can get lots of recognition for your new venture. Remember that the R in GREASE is for "rewarded."
- *Change the cues:* If you're trying to quit a bad habit, make sure you have a positive alternative. If the action that follows the cue, "I need something sweet," is to eat candy, make sure you have an apple in your bag. If the cue is "I'm feeling low," go for a walk instead of getting a sugary drink. This is all about making a plan and having alternatives. Make it easy to keep up with the new habit. Remember the first E in GREASE is for "easy," and the A is for "alternatives."
- *Connect:* Make sure to connect with supporters. Change is a sport team. Ora and I made lots of healthy lifestyle changes together. We talked about our goals and incrementally achieved positive changes such as giving up meat and sugar. We also made a decision to never use physical punishment in parenting. It would have been hard to achieve this goal without mutual support. The S in GREASE is for "supported."

Maintenance   Now that you've started a new routine, it's important to keep it going. Remember that one swallow does not a summer make. Going to the gym once does not make you fit. Most lifestyle changes are marathons and not sprints. You have to make sure that you're ready to manage slips, which will happen. Consider some of these strategies:

- *Challenge negative assumptions:* Most people who have tried to make a change without success invoke myths and clichés to justify their resignation.[14] Common refrains include, "It's all in my genes" and "I've tried it all before, and nothing works." These are fatalistic statements that fly in the face of evidence. A good way to cope with slips and falls is to simply know that they will happen. Expect them, and be ready for them. If you skip going to the gym once, it's not the end of the world. It just means that life is complicated and that plans get disrupted from time to time.

- *Communicate:* Tell your friends and family about your new habit. This is a way to reinforce a healthy lifestyle. Also, ask them to support you in your new pursuit. I (Isaac) tend to be quite neurotic about health and wellness. Of all the changes Ora and I tried to make around health, using the microwave less has been a challenge. This is the next frontier for us. Ora, who seems to think that using the microwave from time to time is not a big deal, is supporting me in trying to give it up altogether. We are being true to the S in GREASE: supported.

You have worked really hard in this chapter. You deserve a break now. Let's look at next steps through a humor lens.

THE LAUGHING SIDE

No amount of awareness or positive connections will do you any good if you do not take the next step in your journey. Remember, the key is to move gradually and slowly. First you define your goal (stop mindless eating), then you break it down into small mini steps (eight donuts a day instead of nine). Then you track your progress using one of the 17,000 apps available for that. Then you review your progress with help from your $450-an-hour coach.

If you decided that you will start a lifestyle change (no nose picking, quit smoking), like most people do as part of their new year's resolution, you must realize that most of them fail miserably. This realization will prevent grave disappointment. The second realization is that you need to read this book again and again.

Clichés

As you can see from previous sections, if you want to modify something about your life, you have to engage drivers of change, but that's not enough. You also have to watch out for barriers, which usually come in the form of clichés. I hate clichés. They're a lazy way to have, and end, a conversation. There are so many problems with clichés. Take for example some popular ones on health and wellness:

- *A crust eaten in peace is better than a banquet partaken in anxiety (Aesop—Fables):* Is the crust whole wheat? Is it gluten-free? Was the banquet vegan, lacto-ovo, kosher, halal, low-purine, high-fiber, or just your mainstream artery-clogging, cholesterol-enhancing, BMI-busting, cardiac-arresting fare? Details please.
- *Early to bed, early to rise, makes a person healthy, wealthy, and wise:* This quote does not tell you anything useful, such as when exactly to go to bed, what time zone we're talking about, how do you define wealthy, and how to account for inflation since Ben Franklin coined the phrase. We scientists need more specifics than generalities.
- *I believe God allows us to make U-turns in life (Mormon website):* Does that rule apply across all states? I don't think God visited Miami lately. If I tried to make some U-turns in Miami, I'd get killed.
- *The man who doesn't relax and hoot a few hoots voluntarily, now and then, is in great danger of hooting hoots standing on his head for the edification of the pathologist and trained nurse a little later on (Elbert Hubbard).* What the %#@?!

And then there are people who are not satisfied with existing clichés but invent their own. A relative's friend recently passed away. The deceased weighed 418 pounds, smoked like a chimney, never exercised in his life, invented the type-A personality, ate like there was no tomorrow, and, *huge surprise*, dropped dead at a young age. Talking to my relative about the untimely dead of his friend he said, "It's all luck in life."

When I make the stupid mistake of talking to people about health and the importance of a vegan diet, proper nutrition, physical activity, and sleep, they often tell me, "We all die in the end." Alternatively, they tell me that "you have to enjoy life" or "it won't kill you to go wild once in a while." The latter is usually accompanied by some story about a distant relative who ate bacon for breakfast, donuts for snack, burgers for lunch, cream puffs for dinner, and lived to be 102. At this point in my writing, many readers begin to feel defensive, so let me drop the subject right now because "better a carnivore reader in hand than a thousand in a vegan market."

Clutter

The reason I move continents every few years is to get rid of junk in our house. I plan on moving every so often to achieve important goals. It's the only way I can manage to dispose of shoes, unfashionable clothes, linen, work documents, pots and pans, and matzo meal for Passover. If we just make a domestic move, my adorable wife Ora wouldn't let me get rid of anything; but a transcontinental move, that's another story. Still, under these circumstances, I have to make sure that I have at least one day of packing when Ora is out of the house. That is my opportunity to throw away things she would never let me touch, such as matzo meal. I make plans for everything, including matzo disposal.

My approach to clutter extermination is to open a big garbage bag and empty most drawers into it for quick disposal. This is the reckless approach. Ora's melancholic approach is to examine old pictures, our son's report card from grade 2, mother's day cards, and immigration applications going back four countries. She peruses everything very slowly and methodically, only to proclaim after hours of careful review that she will make up her mind tomorrow! This attitude is especially problematic in our house, where we have a number of drawers where a lot of procreation takes place. I have proof that if we put in our drawers old paper clips with Mexican coins, they will have sex and produce AAA batteries. This is in the kitchen. In our bedroom, my night table is a site of heresy. In its top drawer, nail clippers have regular intercourse with old socks to produce BIC pencils.

To cope with the growing clutter in our house, we built storage space above the garage. I put in it cans of paint, Memorex tapes from childhood, and old bags. Ora seems to think that I'm hiding there something really important because every day she reminds me that I have to get up there to review the archives of our life, otherwise known as useless junk. We have not seen what's in it since we built it ten years ago. If we're lucky, the termites would have eaten most of it by now. But if my house is any indication, I'll find there matzo meal dating back to the exodus from Egypt.

Nowadays, clutter comes in multiple forms. There is material junk, for which we have to keep buying bigger and bigger houses, and there is digital junk, for which we have to keep buying more and more Dropbox space. There is also print junk, some of which is self-inflicted, and some of which is USPS-inflicted. Every day we get in our mailbox the equivalent of a sequoia tree in the form of Dishnetwork flyers, which manage to impregnate Target catalogues to produce home repair magazines—from the mail delivery time of 2:00 p.m. until I come home at 6:00 p.m. When I contacted USPS to opt out of this environmental catastrophe, I was told that I could not because that would interfere with the free market principles upon which this country was built. Now I leave condoms in the mailbox, hoping to contain the proliferation of unwanted pulp.

Figure 5.1.   Ora hoarding Matzo Meal for Passover.

The self-inflicted kind comes in the form of multiple magazines. I subscribe to a number of weeklies and professional journals so that I can appear smart in social settings. Soon after my arrival in this country, I noticed a lot of people saying things like, "I read in the *New York Times* that . . ." I discovered that name dropping is an important skill in the evolutionary quest for prestige and survival.

In addition to the *Times,* I also subscribe to the *Miami Herald,* mainly because they used to publish my columns until readers got offended by my plastic surgery jokes. But between Dave Barry and Carl Hiassen, you're sure to laugh with the *Herald*, not to mention the real news, which covers anything from a pseudo doctor injecting Fix-a-Flat in a woman's butt to a deranged person running naked through the causeway to bite a homeless guy in the face.

I must read *Miami Today* because they publish my occasional humor column. I also must read *The Economist* for its international coverage and *Time* magazine for The Awesome Column by Joel Stein, and the *New Yorker* for its smart cartoons and for Shouts and Murmurs, which is a column in which one day I'll publish, once the editors discover me. We also used to subscribe to *Newsweek* before its print edition disappeared. Thank God!

To balance the centrist-elitist-neoliberal-right wing tone of *The Economist,* I also subscribe to *The New Internationalist*, which is useful among pretentious left-wing friends because I can say things like, "The intersectionality of oppression." and I can talk about the tragic disappearing of the sub-Saharan cockroach.

I also get seven scientific psychological journals and several educational magazines, plus online versions of the *Tablet*—must keep up with Jewish world—and *Education Week*. In addition, I read *The Chronicle of Higher Education*, mainly to find out if I've been fired. All told, I get on average 12,000 pages of reading material per week. No question, I spend more time managing it all than doing any serious reading, which amount to the *New Yorker* cartoons and The Awesome Column by Stein.

And then, of course, there is the Kindle, with hundreds of books already downloaded, and millions more at my fingertips. I thought of moving again to another continent to streamline my reading commitments, but my Kindle follows me everywhere, as does my email, and LinkedIn and Facebook and Twitter. I should have followed the example of our son who recently deactivated his Facebook account. I, in turn, keep getting inane messages from people in LinkedIn congratulating me on my work anniversary! Not to mention the recurring invitations from three people to join Twitter, which I've done months ago, just to get rid of these annoying invitations, to no avail.

Between material junk, print junk, and digital junk, there is barely any time to fit TV junk into my schedule, for which I now have a DVR, which, get this, I know how to operate. I have a thousand episodes of *The Daily Show*, *The Colbert Report*, and *The Big Bang Theory*, of which we have actually watched three. Between programing the DVR, erasing old programs, and reviewing the TV guide, who has time to watch any TV?

Notes

1. EASE INTO A BETTER LIFE

1. Holt-Lunstad, J., Smith, T., Baker, M., Harris, T., & Stephenson, D. (2015). Loneliness and social isolation as risk factors for mortality: A meta-analytic review. *Perspectives on Psychological Science, 10*(2), 227–37. doi: 10.1177/1745691614568352; Pinker, S. (2014). *The village effect: How face-to-face contact can make us healthier, happier, and smarter.* New York: Random House.

2. DeVito, J. A. (2013). *The interpersonal communication book* (13th ed.). New York: Pearson.

3. Thaler, R., & Sunstein, C. (2008). *Nudge: Improving decisions about health, wealth, and happiness.* New Haven, CT: Yale University Press; Wansink, B. (2014). *Slim by design: Mindless eating solutions.* New York: HarperCollins Publishers.

4. Lyubomirsky, S. (2007). *The how of happiness: A new approach to getting the life you want.* New York: Penguin.

5. Norcross, J. C. (2012). *Changeology: 5 steps to realizing your goals and resolutions.* New York: Simon & Schuster.

2. MASTERING AWARENESS
TO IMPROVE YOURSELF

1. Bannink, F. (2012). *Practicing positive CBT: From reducing distress to building success.* Malden, MA: John Wiley & Sons; Hays, P. A. (2014). *Creating well-being: Four steps to a happier, healthier life.* Washington, DC: American Psychological Association; Peterson, C., & Seligman, M. E. P. (2004). *Character strengths and virtues: A handbook and classification.* Washington, DC: American Psychological Association; Prilleltensky, I. (2016). *The laughing guide to well-being: Using humor and science to become happier and healthier.* Lanham, MD: Rowman & Littlefield.

2. Hayes, S., & Smith, S. (2005). *Get out of your mind and into your life: The new acceptance and commitment therapy.* Oakland, CA: New Harbinger; Harris, R. (2009). *ACT made simple: A quick start to ACT basics and beyond.* Oakland, CA: New Harbinger.

3. Dweck, C. (2016). *Mindset: The new psychology of success.* New York, NY: Random House.

4. Kabat-Zinn, J. (2005). *Full catastrophe living: Using the wisdom of your body and mind to face stress, pain and illness* (15th anniversary ed.). New York, NY: Bantam Dell; Robins, C. J., Keng, S. L., Ekblad, A. G., & Brantley, J. G. (2012). Effects of mindfulness-based stress reduction on emotional experience and expression: A randomized controlled trial. *Journal of Clinical Psychology, 68,* 117–31. doi: 10.1002/jclp.20857

5. Chambers, R., Gullone, E., & Allen, N. B. (2009). Mindful emotion regulation: An integrative review. *Clinical Psychology Review, 29,* 560–72. doi: 10.1016/j.cpr.2009.06.005; Robins, C. J., Keng, S. L., Ekblad, A. G., & Brantley, J. G. (2012). Effects of mindfulness-based stress reduction on emotional experience and expression: A randomized controlled trial. *Journal of Clinical Psychology, 68,* 117–31. doi: 10.1002/jclp.20857; Williams, M., Teasdale, J., Segal, Z., & Kabbat-Zinn, J. (2007). *The mindful way through depression.* New York, NY: Guilford.

6. Freud, S. (1949). *An outline of psychoanalysis* (J. Strachey, Trans.). New York, NY: Norton.

7. Cramer, P. (2006). *Protecting the self: Defense mechanisms in action.* New York, NY: Guilford.

8. Luft, J. (1969). *Of human interaction: The Johari model.* Houston, TX: Mayfield Publishing.

9. Freud, A. (1967). *The ego and the mechanisms of defense* (Revised ed.). New York, NY: International Universities Press.

10. Walburg, & Chiaramello (2015). Link between early maladaptive schemas and defense mechanisms. *Revue Europeenne De Psychologie Appliquee, 65*(5), 221–26.

11. Diehl, M., Chui, H., Hay, E. L., Lumley, M. A., Grühn, D., & Labouvie-Vief, G. (2014). Change in coping and defense mechanisms across adulthood: Longitudinal findings in a European American sample. *Developmental Psychology, 50*(2), 634–48. doi:10.1037/a0033619

12. Metzger, J. A. (2014). Adaptive defense mechanisms: function and transcendence. *Journal of Clinical Psychology, 70*(5), 478–88. doi:10.1002/jclp.22091

13. Sala, M., Testa, S., Pons, F., & Molina, P. (2015). Emotion regulation and defense mechanisms. *Journal of Individual Differences, 36*(1), 19–29.

3. MASTERING INTERACTIONS
TO IMPROVE YOUR RELATIONSHIPS

1. Pinker, S. (2014). *The village effect: How face-to-face contact can make us healthier, happier, and smarter.* New York, NY: Random House.

2. Diener, E., & Biswas-Diener, R. (2008). *Happiness: Unlocking the mysteries of psychological wealth.* Malden, MA: Blackwell.

3. Hawkley, L., & Cacioppo, C. (2010). Loneliness matters: A theoretical and empirical review of consequences and mechanisms. *Annals of Behavioral Medicine, 40*(2), 218–27.

4. Holt-Lunstad, J., Smith, T., Baker, M., Harris, T., & Stephenson, D. (2015). Loneliness and social isolation as risk factors for mortality: A meta-analytic review. *Perspectives on Psychological Science, 10*(2), 227–37. DOI: 10.1177/1745691614568352

5. Lyubomirsky, S. (2007). *The how of happiness: The new approach to getting the life you want.* New York, NY: Penguin.

6. Mikulincer, M., Shaver, P. (2016). *Attachment in adulthood: Structure, dynamics, and change* (2nd ed.). New York, NY: Guilford.

7. Biglan, A. (2015). *The nurture effect: How the science of human behavior can improve our lives and our world.* Oakland, CA: New Horizons; Lieberman, M. (2013). *Social: Why our brains are wired to connect.* New York, NY: Crown.

8. Lieberman, M. (2013). *Social: Why our brains are wired to connect.* New York, NY: Crown.

9. Baumeister, R., & Leary, M. (1995). The need to belong: Desire for interpersonal attachments as a fundamental human motivation. *Psychological Bulletin, 117*(3), 497–529.

10. Lieberman, M. (2013). *Social: Why our brains are wired to connect.* New York, NY: Crown; Pinker, S. (2014). *The village effect: How face-to-face contact can make us healthier, happier, and smarter.* New York, NY: Random House.

11. Lieberman, M. (2013). *Social: Why our brains are wired to connect.* New York, NY: Crown.

12. Powdthavee, N. (2008). Putting a price tag on friends, relatives, and neighbours: Using surveys of life satisfaction to value social relationships. *Journal of Socio-Economics, 37*(4), 1459–80.

13. Kroenke, C., Kubzansky, L., Schernhammer, E., Holmes, M., & Kawachi, I. (2006). Social networks, social support, and survival after breast cancer diagnosis. *Journal of Clinical Oncology: Official Journal of the American Society of Clinical Oncology, 24*(7), 1105–11.

14. Waldinger, R., & Schulz, M. (2016). The long reach of nurturing family environments: links with midlife emotion-regulatory styles and late-life security in intimate relationships. *Psychological Science, 27*(11), 1443–50.

15. Hamblin, J. (2015). The psychological power of altruism, *The Atlantic,* December 30. https://www.theatlantic.com/health/archive/2015/12/altruism-for-a-better-body/422280/

16. Waldinger, R., & Schulz, M. (2016). The long reach of nurturing family environments: Links with midlife emotion-regulatory styles and late-life security in intimate relationships. *Psychological Science, 27*(11), 1443–50.

17. Gottman, J. M, & Gottman, J. (2017). The natural principles of love. *Journal of Family Theory & Review, 9*(1), 7–26.

18. Gottman, J. M., & DeClaire, J. (2001). *The relationship cure: A 5 step guide to strengthening your marriage, family, and friendships* . New York, NY: Crown; Gottman, J. M., & Silver, N. (2000). *The seven principles for making marriage work.* New York, NY: Three Rivers.

19. Gottman, J. M., & Gottman, J. (2017). The natural principles of love. *Journal of Family Theory & Review, 9*(1), 7–26.

20. Baumgardner, R., & Crothers, M. (2009). *Positive psychology.* Upper Saddle River, NJ: Prentice Hall.

21. Rubenstein, C. L., Duff, J., Prilleltensky, I., Jin, Y., Dietz, S., Myers, N. D., & Prilleltensky, O. (2016). Demographic group differences in domain-specific well-being. *Journal of Community Psychology, 44*(4), 499–515. doi:10.1002/jcop.21784

22. Gottman, J. M., & DeClaire, J. (2001). *The relationship cure: A 5 step guide to strengthening your marriage, family, and friendships.* New York, NY: Crown; Gottman, J. M., & Silver, N. (2000). *The seven principles for making marriage work.* New York, NY: Three Rivers.

23. Gottman, J. M. (2015). *Principia amoris: The new science of love.* New York, NY: Routledge.

24. Gottman, J. M., & Gottman, J. (2017). The natural principles of love. *Journal of Family Theory & Review, 9*(1), 7–26.

25. Gottman, J. M, & Gottman, J. (2017). The natural principles of love. *Journal of Family Theory & Review, 9*(1), 7–26.

26. Lopez, S. J., Pedrotti, J. T., & Snyder, C. R. (2015). *Positive psychology: The scientific and practical explorations of human strengths.* (3rd ed.). Thousand Oaks, CA: Sage Publications, Inc.

27. Crocker, J., & Canevello, A. (2016). For better or worse: Compassionate goals create good relationships in good times and bad. In C. Knee & H. Reis (Eds.), *Positive approaches to optimal relationship development* (pp. 211–31). Cambridge: Cambridge University Press. doi:10.1017/CBO9781316212653.012

28. Crocker, J., & Canevello, A. (2016). For better or worse: Compassionate goals create good relationships in good times and bad. In C. Knee & H. Reis (Eds.), *Positive approaches to optimal relationship development* (pp. 211–31). Cambridge, UK: Cambridge University Press. doi:10.1017/CBO9781316212653.012

29. Gable, S. L., Gonzaga, G. C., & Strachman, A. (2006). Will you be there for me when things go right? Supportive responses to positive event disclosures. *Journal of Personality and Social Psychology, 91*, 904–17. doi: 10.1037/0022-3514.91.5.904

30. Deci, E. L., & Ryan, R. M. (2000). The "what" and "why" of goal pursuits: Human needs and the self-determination of behavior. *Psychological Inquiry, 11*, 227–68.

31. Gable, S. (2011). Affiliation and stress. In S. Folkman (Ed.), *The Oxford handbook of health, stress, and coping* (pp. 86–100). New York, NY: Oxford University Press.

32. Pinker, S. (2014). *The village effect: How face-to-face contact can make us healthier, happier, and smarter.* New York, NY: Random House.

33. Kroenke, C., Kubzansky, L., Schernhammer, E., Holmes, M., & Kawachi, I. (2006). Social networks, social support, and survival after breast cancer diagnosis. *Journal of Clinical Oncology: Official Journal of the American Society of Clinical Oncology, 24*(7), 1105–11.

34. Gable, S. (2011). Affiliation and stress. In S. Folkman (Ed.), *The Oxford handbook of health, stress, and coping* (pp. 86–100). New York, NY: Oxford University Press; McKnight, J., & Block, P. (2012). *The abundant community: Awakening the power of families and neighborhoods.* San Francisco, CA: Berrett-Koehler.

35. Grant, A. (2014). *Give and take: Why helping others drives our success.* New York, NY: Penguin.

36. Lyubomirsky, S. (2007). *The how of happiness: The new approach to getting the life you want.* New York, NY: Penguin.

37. Baney, J. (2004). *Guide to interpersonal communication.* New York, NY: Pearson Prentice Hall.

38. Ivey, A., Ivey, M., & Zalaquett, C. (2010). *Intentional interviewing and counseling: Facilitating client development in a multicultural society* (7th ed.). Belmont, CA: Cengage Learning.

39. Brown, K. W., & Ryan, R. M. (2015). A self-determination theory perspective on fostering healthy self-regulation from within and without. In S. Joseph (Ed.), *Positive psychology in practice: Promoting human flourishing in work, health, education, and everyday life* (pp. 139–58). Hoboken, NJ: John Wiley & Sons.

40. Farmer, R. F., & Chapman, A. L. (2016). *Behavioral interventions in cognitive behavior therapy: Practical guidance for putting theory into action* (2nd ed.). Washington, DC: American Psychological Association.

41. Glaser, S., & Glaser, P. A. (2006). *Be quiet be heard: The paradox of persuasion.* Eugene, OR: Communication Solutions Publishing (p. 59).

42. Glaser, S., & Glaser, P. A. (2006). *Be quiet be heard: The paradox of persuasion.* Eugene, OR: Communication Solutions Publishing.

43. Lieberman, M. (2013). *Social: Why our brains are wired to connect.* New York, NY: Crown.

44. Farmer, R. F., & Chapman, A. L. (2016). Behavioral interventions in cognitive behavior therapy: Practical guidance for putting theory into action (2nd ed.). Washington, DC: American Psychological Association.

45. Johnson. D. W., & Johnson, F. P. (2012). *Joining together: Group dynamics and group skills* (11th ed.). Upper Saddle River, NJ: Pearson.

46. Joseph, S. (Ed.). (2015). *Positive psychology in practice: Promoting human flourishing in work, health, education, and everyday life.* Hoboken, NJ: John Wiley & Sons.

47. Crocker, J., Canevello, A., & Brown, A. (2017). Social motivation: Costs and benefits of selfishness and otherishness. *Annual Review of Psychology, 68*, 299–325; Prilleltensky, I. (2014). Meaning-making, mattering, and thriving in community psychology: From co-optation to amelioration and transformation. *Psychosocial Intervention, 23*, 151–54; Prilleltensky, I. (2016). *The laughing guide to well-being: Using humor and science to become happier and healthier.* Lanham, MD: Rowman & Littlefield.

48. Gable, S. L., Gonzaga, G. C., & Strachman, A. (2006). Will you be there for me when things go right? Supportive responses to positive event disclosures. *Journal of Personality and Social Psychology, 91*, 904–17. doi: 10.1037/0022-3514.91.5.904

4. MASTERING CUES TO
IMPROVE YOUR SURROUNDINGS

1. Ariely, D. (2009). *Predictably irrational: The hidden forces that shape our decisions.* New York, NY: HarperCollins.
2. Thaler, R., & Sunstein, C. (2008). *Nudge: Improving decisions about health, wealth, and happiness.* New Haven, CT: Yale University Press.
3. Martins, C. M., & Vallen, B. (2014). The impact of holiday eating cues on self-regulatory bolstering for dieters and non-dieters. *Psychology & Health, 29*(4), 999–1013. doi: 10.1080/08870446.2014.900682
4. Ariely, D. (2009). *Predictably irrational: The hidden forces that shape our decisions.* New York, NY: HarperCollins.
5. Wansink, B. (2014). *Slim by design: Mindless eating solutions.* New York, NY: HarperCollins Publishers.
6. Asch, S. E. (1956). Studies of independence and conformity. A minority of one against a unanimous majority. *Psychological Monographs, 70(9),* 1–70.
7. Cialdini, R. (1993). *Influence: The psychology of persuasion.* New York, NY: Quill; Thaler, R., & Sunstein, C. (2008). *Nudge: Improving decisions about health, wealth, and happiness.* New Haven, CT: Yale University Press.
8. Steele, C. M., & Aronson, J. (1995). Stereotype threat and the intellectual test performance of African-Americans. *Journal of Personality and Social Psychology, 69,* 797–811; Steele, C. (2010). *Whistling Vivaldi: How stereotype affect us and what we can do.* New York, NY: Norton.
9. Lobel, T. (2014). *Sensation: The new science of physical intelligence.* New York, NY: Simon & Schuster.
10. Cialdini, R. (1993). *Influence: The psychology of persuasion.* New York, NY: Quill.
11. Norcross, J. C. (2012). *Changeology: 5 steps to realizing your goals and resolutions.* New York, NY: Simon & Schuster.
12. Dolan, P. (2014). *Happiness by design: Change what you do, not how you think.* New York, NY: Hudson Street Press; Papies, E. K., & Hamstra, P. (2010). Goal priming and eating behavior: Enhancing self-regulation by environmental cues. *Health Psychology, 29*(4), 384–88. doi:10.1037/a0019877
13. Dolan, P. (2014). *Happiness by design: Change what you do, not how you think.* New York, NY: Hudson Street Press.
14. Baumeister, R. F., & Tierney, J. (2011). *Willpower: Rediscovering the greatest human strength.* New York, NY: Penguin; McGonigal, K. (2012). *The willpower instinct: Why self-control works, why it matters, and how you can get more of it.* New York, NY: Penguin; Papies, E. K., & Hamstra, P. (2010). Goal priming and eating behavior: Enhancing self-regulation by environmental cues. *Health Psychology, 29*(4), 384–88. doi:10.1037/a0019877
15. Wansink, B. (2014). *Slim by design: Mindless eating solutions.* New York, NY: HarperCollins.
16. Ulrich, R. (1984). View through a window may influence recovery from surgery. *Science, 224,* 420–21.
17. Thaler, R., & Sunstein, C. (2008). *Nudge: Improving decisions about health, wealth, and happiness.* New Haven, CT: Yale University Press.
18. Ariely, D. (2009). *Predictably irrational: The hidden forces that shape our decisions.* New York, NY: HarperCollins.
19. Cialdini, R. (1993). *Influence: The psychology of persuasion.* New York, NY: Quill.

5. MASTERING A PLAN TO MAKE IT STICK

1. Evers, A., Klusmann, V., Schwarzer, R., & Heuser, I. (2012). Adherence to physical and mental activity interventions: Coping plans as a mediator and prior adherence as a moderator. *British Journal of Health Psychology, 17*(3), 477–91. doi:10.1111/j.2044-8287.2011.02049.x; Kiernan, M., Brown, S. D., Schoffman, D. E., Lee, K., King, A. C., Taylor, C. B., & Perri, M. G. (2013). Promoting healthy weight with "stability skills first": A randomized trial. *Journal of Consulting & Clinical Psychology, 81*(2), 336–46. doi:10.1037/a0030544; Lange, D., Richert, J., Koring, M., Knoll, N., Schwarzer, R., & Lippke, S. (2013). Self-regulation prompts can increase fruit consumption: A one-hour randomised controlled online trial. *Psychology & Health, 28*(5), 533–45. doi:10.1080/08870446.2012.751107
2. King, L. A. (2000). The health benefits of writing about life goals. *Personality & Social Psychology Bulletin, 27*(7), 798–807. doi: 10.1177/0146167201277003
3. Lyubomirsky, S. (2007). *The how of happiness: A new approach to getting the life you want.* New York, NY: Penguin.
4. Norcross, J. C. (2012). *Changeology: 5 steps to realizing your goals and resolutions.* New York, NY: Simon & Schuster; Weick, K. (1984). Small wins. *American Psychologist, 39*(1), 40–49.
5. Watson, D. L., & Tharp, R. G. (2014). *Self-directed behavior: Self-modification for personal adjustment* (10th ed.). Belmont, CA: Cengage Learning.
6. Bowen, S., & Marlatt, A. (2009). Surfing the urge: Brief mindfulness-based intervention for college student smokers. *Psychology of Addictive Behaviors, 23*(4), 666–71. doi: 10.1037/a0017127

7. Wing, R. R., & Jeffery, R. W. (1999). Benefits of recruiting participants with friends and increasing social support for weight loss and maintenance. *Journal of Consulting and Clinical Psychology, 67*(1), 132–138. doi:10.1037/0022-006X.67.1.132

8. Adriannse, M. A., Gollwitzer, P. M., De Ridder, D. T. D., De Wit, J. B. F., & Kroese, F. M. (2011). Breaking habits with implementation intentions: A test of underlying processes. *Personality and Social Psychology Bulletin, 37*, 502–13. doi: 10.1177/0146167211399102; McGonigal, K. (2012). *The willpower instinct: Why self-control works, why it matters, and how you can get more of it.* New York, NY: Penguin; Wiedemann, A. U., Lippke, S., Reuter, T., Ziegelmann, J. P., & Schwarzer, R. (2011). How planning facilitates behaviour change: Additive and interactive effects of a randomized controlled trial. *European Journal of Social Psychology, 41*(1), 42–51. doi:10.1002/ejsp.724

9. Watson, D. L., & Tharp, R. G. (2014). *Self-directed behavior: Self-modification for personal adjustment* (10th ed.). Belmont, CA: Cengage Learning.

10. Norcross, J. C. (2012). *Changeology: 5 steps to realizing your goals and resolutions.* New York, NY: Simon & Schuster; Witkiewitz, K., & Marlatt, G. A. (2004). Relapse prevention for alcohol and drug problems: That was Zen, this is Tao. *American Psychologist, 59*, 224–35. doi: 10.1037/0003-066X.59.4.224

11. Prilleltensky, I., & Prilleltensky, O. (2006). *Promoting well-being: Linking personal, organizational, and community change.* Hoboken, NJ: Wiley.

12. Ludovici, A. (2014). *Change your mind, change your health.* Pompton Plains, NJ: New Page Books; Norcross, J. C. (2012). *Changeology: 5 steps to realizing your goals and resolutions.* New York, NY: Simon & Schuster; Prochaska, J., Norcross, J., & DiClemente, C. (1994). *Changing for good.* New York: Avon Books.

13. Norcross, J. C. (2012). *Changeology: 5 steps to realizing your goals and resolutions.* New York, NY: Simon & Schuster.

14. Norcross, J. C. (2012). *Changeology: 5 steps to realizing your goals and resolutions.* New York, NY: Simon & Schuster.

Index

About the Authors

Dr. Isaac Prilleltensky is professor of educational and psychological studies at the University of Miami, where he also serves as vice provost for institutional culture. He holds the Erwin and Barbara Mautner Chair in Community Well-Being. From 2006 to 2017, he was dean of the School of Education and Human Development at the University of Miami. He has published nine books and over one hundred and twenty scholarly papers and book chapters. He is the recipient of the Distinguished Contribution to Theory and Research Award, and the John Kalafat Applied Community Psychology Award, both from the Division of Community Psychology of the American Psychological Association (APA). He is also the recipient of the lifetime achievement award of the Prevention Section of the Division of Counseling Psychology of APA. In 2015, he received an award from the National Newspaper Association for his humor writing. Isaac was born in Argentina and has lived and worked in Israel, Canada, Australia, and the United States. He lives in Miami with his amazing wife, Dr. Ora Prilleltensky. Their son, Matan, lives in New York City. Isaac can be reach at isaac@miami.edu.

Dr. Ora Prilleltensky obtained her doctorate in counseling psychology from the Ontario Institute of Studies in Education (OISE) at the University of Toronto. She is the former director of the major in human and social development at the University of Miami and has taught various graduate and undergraduate courses. Prior to moving to Miami, Ora taught at Vanderbilt's Peabody College. She has also worked in a variety of clinical settings, including a child guidance clinic, a university counseling center and a rehabilitation hospital. Ora has muscular dystrophy and uses a power wheelchair. Her research interests include disability studies and the promotion of well-being. She is the author of *Motherhood and Disability: Children and Choices* and the co-author of *Promoting Well-being: Linking Personal, Organizational and Community Change* and *The Laughing Guide to Change: Using Humor and Science to Master your Behaviors, Emotions, and Thoughts.* Ora is on the board of Research and Reform for Children in Court. She has also served on Miami–Dade County's Commission on Disability Issues. Ora can be reached at ora@miami.edu.